Les Dawson's
Secret Notebooks

Gags, Routines, Sketches and Scripts from

Les Dawson's
Secret Notebooks

Selected and introduced by

Tracy Dawson

BOOKS

First published in Great Britain in 2007 by JR Books,
10 Greenland Street, London NW1 0ND
www.jrbooks.com

A catalogue record for this book is available from the British Library.

ISBN 978-1-906217-19-8

1 3 5 7 9 10 8 6 4 2

Printed by MPG Books Ltd, Bodmin, Cornwall

Contents

For Charlotte, as Les would have wished.

Acknowledgements

There are a number of people I wish to thank for their friendship in the years since Les died. First and foremost, I would like to express my appreciation to John Chadwick for his continued loyalty and support to me and my family. My thanks also to my dear friends Len Rawciffe, Mo Moorland, Jean Smith and Barbara Smart; to John Lavelle and Ruth for their generous hospitality and the use of their office; to Charlotte Harris of George Davies for her legal guidance; to Anthony Harkavy for his wise and friendly counsel; to all Les's old mates at the Water Rats; and of course to Les's many fans who have continued to write and keep in touch over the years.

I owe a special thanks to my publishers JR Books, and in particular to their Senior Editor Lesley Wilson, to designer Richard Mason, and to Lucian Randall for his help in sifting and organising the dizzying amount of material that Les left behind. I would also like to place on record my thanks and appreciation for the friendship built up over the last 20 or so years with Carole and Jeremy Robson, who published a number of Les's books at their old company Robson Books, and are the publishers of this one.

And above all, my thanks must go to Les – for making this possible and all the laughter and love he gave us all.

<u>Introduction</u>

Les loved to write, it was a real passion. When he was working and touring, he would scribble away in his notebooks, honing his routines, filling page after page with gags and ripostes – often on one theme – which he developed and played with and improvised on. When he was at home, he would shut himself away in his study, and the red-hot pages would fly from his battered old typewriter – comic novels, monologues, scripts, pantomime lines, gags, whatever. Yet it all looked so effortless when he went on stage, or sat opposite Terry Wogan or Michael Parkinson, the jokes following one another like bullets so that even those seasoned interviewers had to fight to get a word in or hold back their laughter.

But it wasn't effortless, and like all great comics Les could have his down moments, when self-doubt intruded... though never for long. For Les was the ultimate perfectionist, and he really worked at everything he did – developing, changing, polishing – as can be seen from the pages of jokes on different themes that appear in this book. And to sit at the piano, dead-pan, and play off-key, to just miss those notes, as he loved to do, well you have to be a really good musician to do that, and he was. At the end of a busy day, Les loved to sit down at the Grand piano in our living room and would play for hours, mostly jazz which he adored. All in perfect tune!

Of course, Les loved to send things up, that dead-pan delivery disguising his mischievous intent, as all who remember his *Blankety Blank* appearances will recall all too well. And he did this too in his stage routines and monologues, as can be seen here, or on such radio spots as Dr Rhubarb's Corner – Les, the ultimate agony aunt! Then, of course, there are the unforgettable Cissie and Ada sketches with the wonderful Roy Baraclough, which Les loved, and the many other 'spots' and appearances.

Les had many friends in the business, and he greatly valued his membership of the Water Rats, the show business charity that raises money for performers who have fallen on hard times, as well as for other charities. In 1985, Les was made King Rat – an honour he cherished. Whenever he could he went to their lunches or dinners, and when he couldn't attend for some reason he sent them hilarious letters of apology which they relished and read out. A few of these letters are included here.

Les came into my life at the end of 1986. We met at the Saint Ives Hotel in Lytham St Anne's, where I was working. It was a low time in Les's life, and in mine too. He had just lost his wife Meg to cancer, as he movingly describes in his autobiography *No Tears for the Clown*, and my mother had also just died of cancer. We found ourselves talking about the treatment they

The evening of our wedding, May 6th 1989.

had received and what we had both been through. It seemed to form a bond. We met again when we were both working for the Scanner Appeal Charity to raise money for Blackpool's Victoria Hospital. Les was fronting the charity and helped raise the first million pounds for the scanner. We got engaged in 1988, and married a year later at the White Church in Lytham. We had a glorious seven years together, crowned by the birth of our lovely daughter Charlotte whom Les adored.

With Les, what you saw was what you got. He always saw the funny side of the serious. He had brilliance, wisdom and a sense of his own worth, and he always treated people in precisely the same way, with genuine interest and concern. That's what made him so special, and so popular.

Les was particularly proud of his Northern roots. We had a flat in London at one point, when he was working there a lot, and we toyed with the idea of moving nearer to London as he had many friends and colleagues there. Together we looked round a number of lovely Southern villages, but Les always ended up saying, 'There's nowhere in England nicer than Lytham St Anne's. It's sheer heaven!' He felt this so strongly that when he was appearing in a show in Bournemouth, and I was heavily pregnant with Charlotte and about to go into labour, Les panicked at the thought of having our child born in the South and hired a jet to fly me back to Manchester. On landing there I was rushed to St Mary's Hospital where Charlotte was born very shortly after.

Les as a proud dad.

Les died suddenly of a heart attack in 1993. He had suffered two previous attacks, the first when he was about to go on stage at the Blackpool Opera House, the second when he was appearing at the Wimbledon Theatre. After the first attack he had to take two months off, during which time he wrote a book. I'm sure that if he were alive today he would spend a lot of his time writing. He took his writing very seriously.

The last interview Les gave, about a week before he died, was on psychiatrist Anthony Claire's fascinating BBC Radio 4 programme *In the Psychiatrist's Chair*. It was the most colourful and honest interview I ever heard Les give. Indeed, Dr Claire was so impressed by Les that he wanted to take him to meet some of his patients who were suffering from depression, so that Les could talk to them, bring some laughter and joy to their lives, and convey his belief in the healing power of laughter. Alas, it was not to be.

When Les died, he left behind a cupboard full of fabulously funny material, some of it typed, much in his own handwriting, which he had always told me was part of our daughter Charlotte's legacy. So this book is very much for Charlotte. I am particularly delighted that it includes a special note Les wrote specially for her.

Les may have been a great comic, but there's no dodging the fact that he was not the world's greatest typist, and mistakes often spattered the pages almost as prolifically as his jokes: he never took to or could cope with the word processor I bought him. So to help the reader, we've re-typed some of the material to make it easier to read, as well as reproducing some of his original pages to give the real flavour of Les, mistakes and all. Also, Les loved to re-work and re-angle tried and trusted gags into new contexts, so if you spot a slight repetition here or there, forgive him! He also tended to head his pieces Piano Spots, Monologues, Cabaret, Radio, Openers, or whatever, and by and large we've followed his lead, loosely grouping things.

Above all, I hope that the real Les comes through these pages, and that they make you laugh – as if Les was coming out for one more encore. That would cheer him no end!

Tracy Dawson, September 2007

My name is Les Dawson –
that's a stage name actually. I was christened
Friday Dawson because when my father saw me
he said to my mother,
'I think we'd better call it a day.'

Thank you ..... but there's no need for applause,
I ask only of you a little sympathy and if humanely possible,
a ten yard start.

You're probably wondering who I am, it's not
surprising, because I'm wondering who I am. I've been trying
for so long to make my name in this business, I've forgotten
what it is now.

Judging by the startled expression on some of your
faces, you're obviously baffled as to what I do by way of
an act, it's understandable.... it's got me bothered as well.
As a matter of fact, I am a comedian, I thought I'd tell
you now what I am because between you and I, I don't like
secrets.

*Les would tailor his material for different occasions – his own shows, guest
appearances and commercial work such as after dinner speeches.*

Law and order monologue

I'd like to talk to you tonight about law and order. What is happening to our
society today? Riots, vandalism, muggings, where's it all going to end? Of
course, police methods are different now. In my young days, if the local bobby
saw us on the street corner, he'd come over and give us a friendly piece of
advice. Then he'd take us around the back and beat the living daylights out
of us.

But I came from a very poor neighbourhood. Well, it was so bad, vandals
had to supply their own phone boxes. And petty theft was rife. It got to the
stage where we had to brand the greenfly. Not that things have improved
much. Why, only the other night, the mother-in-law had a nasty experience. A
burglar broke down the front door – trying to get out. But I think her worst
experience was when she got married. She left the church, raised her veil
and got done for indecent exposure.

Stand up

There have been many great love stories – Romeo and Juliet, Dante and
Beatrice, Hero and Leander, Des O'Connor and Des O'Connor, but they pale
into insignificance when compared to the romance of my great grandfather,
Tobias Dawson. A wonderful man, he stood six-foot-four, never smoked, never
drank, never went out with loose women and made all his own frocks. In
the spring of 1898, he was banished by the family to Canada after an ugly
incident involving a Burmese juggler and a cocker spaniel in the Cocoa Rooms
and Thermal Baths, Crewe. Nobody knows what happened but the juggler got
six months and the dog had its licence endorsed.

Les at the Variety Club of Great Britain with Danny La Rue and Dame Vera Lynn.

Spot

Last week, I stood in the smoke-blackened ruins of what was once an edifice of baroque magnificence – the Royal Opera House, Sandbach. I confess that tears sprang unbidden to my eyes as I surveyed the council wreckers at work, toiling to clear that famous site in order to make way for three blocks of grey cement flats and a relief sewage pipe to Wrexham. Anger throbbing through my whole being caused a faintness and I stumbled into a gaping hole. I found myself sprawled in a spray of choking dust, clutching an aged, worm-riddled oaken beam. To ascertain my position, I struck a match in the acrid gloom and there on the beam was etched the legend 'Hamilton De Quincy was here, 1952.'

The name rolled the passage of time back across the gulf of memories. Hamilton De Quincy, real name, Alf Broadbottom – my uncle. The family scoffed at him because he was out of work so often, every time they built a new labour exchange, they called him in as a consultant. He started his acting career with the Giggleswick Repertory Company, playing little Lord Fauntleroy. He played that part for fifteen years then got sacked when his tights split. Broken-hearted, he auditioned for a part in the Hunckback of Notre Dame, but unfortunately he got cramp and fell off Charles Laughton's back.

For a time he toured with a parrot that did impressions of Lloyd George, Lillian Gish and Victor Mature. My father saw him one day dressed in filthy rags, he was thin and pale and quite destitute, and he was holding a grubby tray in his arms. Father said, 'What are you doing, Hamilton?' He said, 'Selling lucky mascots.' My dad was upset, he said, 'But you were doing so well with our parrot. Where is it?' Hamilton said, 'I had to eat it.' Dad said, 'You ate your parrot? What did it taste like?' He said, 'Turkey. That parrot could imitate anybody.'

Things went from bad to worse for Hamilton De Quincy when he went on tour. The night I saw it at the Gaiety Theatre, Gateshead, the place was so empty, they were hunting stags in the balcony. I lost touch with my uncle De

Quincy for quite some time, then I heard that he was in a Jewish pantomime called *Abe's in a Wood*. He sang the hit song, 'I Did it Oy Vay'.

Then winsome fate appeared to call off the vendetta of ill fortune and my uncle was offered a part in a dramatic play. He only had two lines to deliver, but they were important to the production to highlight the stark drama of the piece. That night in his humble lodgings in a Whitechapel slum, he stalked across the room, declaiming in his rich fruity tones that pierced the damp, musty air: 'It is... It is...' For two months he worked on his miniscule redition. He would peer into shop windows to catch his reflection and he would boom, 'It is!'

The opening of the play arrived. The glittering audience filed into the foyer of the theatre, the hum of conversation increased in anticipation, wreaths of cigar smoke drifted in aimless spirals towards the sparkling chandeliers and waiters scurried with decanters, weaving twixt elegant groups of critical theatrical habitues. Soon the house lights dimmed, latecomers were ushered to their seats, nervous coughs were muffled in expensive handkerchiefs and the velvet curtain rose to reveal the majesty of the stage setting. Onto to the podium strode Hamilton De Quincy, bedecked in his doublet and hose, his dirk poised in his gloved hand.

A hush settled on the auditorium as he mounted a dais to deliver his two words. Flushed with the occasion, Hamilton took a deep breath and roared, 'Is it!' Pandemonium ensued. He was dragged off the stage by the irate stage manager who shook him by the throat and snarled, 'You're fired!' Hamilton said, 'You can't sack me.' The stage manager said, 'Why not?' He said, 'I know the part backwards.'

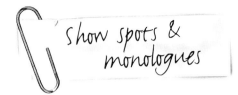

Dennis Waterman: Just to contemplate this mission is pain beyond belief...
I'm up against a man who will sink to any depths...
whose very presence instils revulsion... whose dire deeds
are placing the entire nation in peril.

Les: You mean...

Dennis: Yes. I'm going on *The Les Dawson Show*.

Les: [STANDS] Right, that's enough! CUT! Stop everything!
FINISH! I didn't think that was funny! That's the last
time   you ever come on my show!

Dennis: Can I have that in writing?

Les: What for? You probably couldn't read it.

Comedian: A fine humourist who is definately going places next year he's doing
pantomime in the Orkneys.

Actor: He's played Shakespeare and everytime he's lost.

Actress: ~~Xxxxxxxxxxxxxxxx~~ What makes a magnifivent actress? If you find
out ~~xxxxxxxxxxx~~ would you please drop........ a line?

Singer(Male)   ....what a singer...the only man 1 know with air brakes on his
tonsils.

Singer(Female)   Her voice once cracked a glass...not a wine glass, a triplex
windscreen

This Calendar *monologue celebrated the long-running ITV regional news programme. The late Richard Whiteley was one of its main presenters and a close friend of Les.*

Speech

We are all here today to commemorate ten years of the programme *Calendar*, the news programme that is to show business what Julie Andrews was to *Deep Throat*. Ten years, that's a decade. It's certainly decayed Richard Whitely, who as you all know is the thinking man's Jess Yates. Richard once bought me a drink in the bar – I'm not saying it was a rare event but when he pulled a pound note out of his pocket the Queen bit his thumb.

The main reason why I was glad to asked along here today is because I worked for Yorkshire Television for eight years and I must say the heads of the company couldn't do enough for me... so they never bothered. They gave me a dressing room to myself. I'm not saying the room was in a mess but vandals broke in one night and decorated it. After every show when I received my cheque, I took it straight to the bank. Well, I had to, it was too small to go by itself.

I have many happy memories of my stay with Yorkshire Television. I remember with affection the canteen, known to all and sundry as Heartburn Alley, it's difficult to describe what the food was like, but the mice used to set their own traps. Now, of course, Yorkshire is one of the giant TV companies producing popular programmes like *Emmerdale Farm*, which is a sort of *Peyton Place* with manure.

You've never come across a pair like 'em... They undressed last week without drawing the bedroom curtains and a peeping Tom across the road gave himself up... Before I leave you I'd like to conclude by playing for you my latest recording for Pye... It should do extremely well it's got a four inch crust...

I have never ogled the television with any degree of avidity,
mainly because our old set takes so long too warm up, we get
"Stars on Sunday" on Wednesday. Also, it possess a very small
screen...so small in fact, if they ever show "Snow White and the
Seven Dwarfs" we'll only get Grumpy on ours. I have toyed with the
idea of buying or renting a more up to date model, but frankly, they
cost the very earth and in no way will 1 delve into my liqueur
fund. No, we will have to make do with it, despite the fact that
the instructions for maintenance are written in Latin.
Having said all that, 1 must confess that the television saga:"Roots"
made an enormous impact on me spiritually...so much so, 1 burned, nay
ached, to discover something of my heritage, and so, 1 journeyed
forth to Somerset House to seek the Dawson family tree, which 1
rather fancied would turn out to be a diseased elm.
I was wrong. The Dawson Tree turned out to be a sort of Weeping Willow.
It was all there in the musty volumes, an historic rota of potential
arsonists and muggers. To my chagrin, there was evidence to suggest that
one of my ancestors had been an active Liberal in Rhyl.
Having recovered from that blow, 1 discovered that the Family had
sprang from Nordic loins in the shape of one Elric the Peculiar, the
only viking ever to land in Gateshead waving a white flag. He married
Winnie Winifred, the eldest daughter of a lame thatcher, and
she sold chamber pots to the Iceni tribe...She became well known and
in Flamborough, was refered to as:"Winnie The Po!"

He wasn't a bad fellow, Dad, he said to me once, 'Listen son one day I'll take
you away from all this squalor and we'll live in Venice and ride up and
down the Grand Canal on a Gorgonzola'. I said, 'But Daddy, that's a lump of
cheese.' He said, 'Who the hell cares as long as it doesn't leak...'

   Still that was a long time ago and the only time my childhood is mentioned
is when the wife's mother starts sneering at me... She's a real snob that
woman... She's always on about what a good education she had. She said to
me, 'When I was a girl at school, I had Algebra every day'. I said, 'That's
nothing we had Tapioca...'

Dawson and Friends

16 March
Final show

[SING: 'O WHAT A BEAUTIFUL MORNING']

My wife came upstairs and gave me my breakfast in bed this morning. She
threw it straight from the pan. I didn't mind. It's not the first time I've had
poached egg on quilt. I know why she was annoyed, it was because I'd spilt
hot cocoa down her nightdress. It serves me right for wearing it. I got up and
did my morning exercises – up 1, 2, 3, down 1, 2, 3 – then my other eyelid.
Oh, I don't look it but I'm as fit as a fiddle and every artery as solid as a
rock. In my youth I was a boxer. I wasn't very good, in fact I was carried out
of the ring so often I had handles sewn on my shorts. I was knocked out so
cold in one fight they picked me off the floor with ice tongs. I'm healthy
enough, all I suffer from is indigestion. I went to the nurse here at Yorkshire
TV. I said, 'What's good for wind?' She gave me a kite. Anyway, I got dressed,
went into the mother-in-law's bedroom. She was sat up in bed with tears in
her eyes listening to a record of Hitler's speeches. She didn't see me at first,
she was smacking the cat with her iron cross...

Page three

One night on the beach, the wife turned to me. She said, 'Do you know, my dearest heart, that ever since we have been married you have always reminded me of the sea?' I said, 'In what way, my angel? Do you mean that I'm wild, restless and untamed?' She said, 'No. You make me sick.'

Mind you, it's no secret that we've never got on. She said to me the other night, 'You're no good to me. I want a man who can thrill me like Rock Hudson, hold me like Kirk Douglas and make my blood boil like Marlon Brando. What can you do?' I said, 'Go and fetch my teeth while I bite you like Lassie.'

It was our wedding anniversary last week. Fourteen years. I couldn't believe it was that long. For the life of me I don't remember breaking two mirrors. She said, 'Let's celebrate. Go in the backyard and kill a couple of chickens.' I said, 'Why blame them for what happened fourteen years ago?' Like most women, she's always trying to be superior. She's always boasting that she had five 'O' levels in algebra. I wouldn't care but she doesn't speak a word of it now.

Last time I was up here I took the wife out for a meal in … you know, that's where they take fish and chips home in a briefcase. When they win at bingo round there, they don't shout, 'House,' they stand up, wave a glove and say, 'Maison.'

I got talking to a fellow round there. I said, 'It's nice round here, what are the rates like?' He said, 'We don't have rates, just mice.' What a snob – he said, 'I have the cleanest cat in the district. If it does anything in the garden, it fills the hole in straight away.' I said, 'All cats do that.' He said, 'What, with a shovel?'

Anyway, the wife and I sat down in the restaurant. What a place – it was so posh, they had filtered tips on the smoked salmon and spats on the pigs feet. The waiter came over. He said, 'Have you got a reservation?' I said, 'What the hell do you think I am, a flaming red Indian? He looked at the wife and he said, 'Well, you must be a brave.'

*Les with the Roly Polys, a dancing troupe originated by Les for one of his shows,
who went on to become a household name.*

Show spots & monologues

Show four

Main spot

The blood that flows in the veins of every Briton is the plasma of history. Our heritage was forged in the crucible of the great warrior tribes. The Norsemen, the Saxons, the Goths, the Normans, the Jutes and the Angles have all contributed to our traditional character.

Every family in this sceptred isle is a monument to those sturdy races of long ago and after watching that television saga, Roots, I decided to trace my family tree, which turned out to be a sort of stunted weeping willow.

[CHART HERE SHOWING DIFFERENT FACES, ALL COSMO SMALLPIECE]

The Dawson dynasty began with Elric the Peculiar, the first Viking to get mugged in Gateshead. To prove their manhood, young Vikings had to fight a rampant wild boar and sleep with a maiden. Unfortunately, Elric was deaf and he appeared in the camp torn and bleeding, dragging his leg and shouting, 'Where's the maiden I have to fight with?'

As vice chairman of the Mordecai Appeal fund for the preservation of the Lesser Horned Morecamble whelk, I feel that I should lay our case before you. This delightful denizen of our shores is rapidly becoming extinct because pollution is making it crosseyed...This leads to frustration in trying to mate and in one instance a mature whelk ruptured himself trying to mount a discarded yoghout carton...A horrified trawler skipper testified that he had witnessed four whelks using a crab for a gang bang... We have tried to fit them with national health glasses but we do have a problem there...no ears. to keep them on. Our basic aim is to open a chain of clinics from Newport to ɪɪɪɪɪɪɪ Rotherham, where whelks can be fitted with contact lenses, have steam baths and their hair done...Twice a month whelks who are suicidal, are taken by coach to the Lake District to see the Polish Morris Dancers at winderemere, they thorouly enjoy it and as they ɪɪɪɪɪɪɪɪɪɪɪ love humming to an accordian. it really is a thrill to see a happy whelk whistle at tins of tuna fish in Kendal, and even the deaf ones seen to enjoy lip reading. Please help us all you can by giving a small donation directly to me Les Dawson C/O My house.

Les as randy Cosmo Smallpiece: 'Knickers, knackers, knockers.'

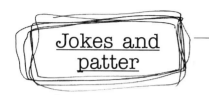
She was so ugly, her birth certificate was an X.

Good fortune has pased me by so many times that I walk along
giving a slowing down signal.

They tell us parents we should love our kids. We should kiss them
before they go to bed at night. But who's going to stay up until
they've gone to bed?

Delightful cottage nestling in the country with a small swimming
pool at the bottom, old man lying there.
'Isn't it wonderful how he can hold his breath?'
'Not really' said his wife, 'He's been down there a month'

I've not always been a comedian. There was a time when
I had regular meals.

"I WOULD'NT SAY THE SHIP WAS OLD" — BUT !!!

1 THEY STARTED IT WITH A WHIP

2 THE FUNNEL WAS THATCHED

3 DIDN'T LIKE THE CAPTAIN - CALLED ME JIM LAD AND HIS PARROT SMELT.

4 THE CAPTAIN HAD NIGHTMARES ABOUT THE ARMADA.

5 THE PORTHOLES WORE GLASSES (CONTACT LENSES)

6 THE RATS RUNNING ABOUT WORE POWDERED WIGS

7 THEY HELD A COMPETITION TO GUESS THE SPEED OF THE SHIP - AND THE WINNER GOT A SLAVE

Cissie and Ada

Cissie Braithwaite (Coronation Street's Roy Barraclough) and Ada Shufflebottom (Les) were two old dears forever discussing their personal 'lady's problems' – Les quickly mouthing the more private aspects silently and pushing up his enormous bosom in embarrassment.

Cissie and Ada

Ada: I can't take much more, Cissie.

Cissie: What's the matter with you? We've only been here two days.

Ada: I should never have listened to you. Health farm indeed! My stomach thinks my throat's cut.

Cissie: If you want to lose weight and get back into a junior miss frock, you'll have to grin and bear it. I mean look at the state of you in those shorts. Your skin's so stretched, every time you bend down your hair net falls off.

Ada: Well, that's nice, I must say. I can't take any more of it. Dinner last night was three strands of watercress and a prune.

Cissie: Now, come on, Ada. Persevere and you'll come up trumps.

Ada: The prunes are seeing to that. I've spent so much time on the loo I'm being charged ground rent.

Cissie: If we want to be beautiful, we have to suffer. Everybody here is in the same boat. Look at that man last night at the next table. Did you notice his corpulence?

Ada: I'm too hungry to think of that.

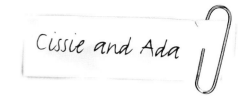

Cissie: There was hardly anything on his plate. Did you see his bean sprout?

Ada: It's a wonder he's got the energy.

Cissie: Oh, Ada, you are pig ignorant at times. Pull yourself together and think that one day soon you'll be able to get into a bikini.

Ada: I'd sooner get into a steak and kidney pie with a suet crust and big, lovely fat chips soaked in gravy.

Cissie: Stop it, Ada, you're cracking up!

Ada: And you call yourself a friend. I'm starving, Cissie. [LOUD TUM NOISE] Listen to that, I've got more gas in me than the North Sea.

Cissie: Keep your chin up, love, it'll all come out right in the end.

Ada: I want something to go down the top first. I don't know why I bothered trying to become slim and attractive at my age. It won't do any good. Bert's past it now – the only time he gets a gleam in his eye is when he gets a shock off the electric blanket.

Cissie: Don't you kid yourself, Ada, men never change. Last week my Leonard saw me in the nude as I stepped out of the bath. I said, 'What do you think after all these years, Leonard?' He kissed me and gave me my wedding dress and said, 'Let's relive our honeymoon.' You should try it, Ada, it might surprise you.

Ada: I did try it once. I walked up to Bert with nowt on and said, 'What do you think?' He said, 'It wants ironing.'

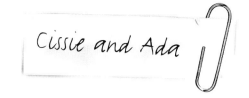

Cissie and Ada

Cissie: Let me freshen your cup of tea, Ada love, and do try a piece of my home-baked Wiltshire herbal flan.

Ada: Thank you, chuck. Very nice... spicy.

Cissie: Our Glenda's friend, a country-bred lady of some quality, gave her the original recipe, which I am led to believe was first concocted by a cook in a sort of monastic hospice. What are you spitting it out for?

Ada: Dirty devils.

Cissie: What are you talking about, Ada?

Ada: As if you didn't know. Suppose the horse had a disease?

Cissie: That's it, Ada! Just how pig ignorant can you get. A hospice, you fool, is a special place to succour the suffering.

Ada: Well, I didn't know, did I? Typical of you, throwing your education at me.

Cissie: You had the same chances that I had, it just that I paid attention to the lessons given. That's why I did so well in algebra.

Ada: Well, what good did that do you? You can't speak a word of it now.

Left: Roy Barraclough as Ada Shufflebottom and Les as Cissie Braithwaite.
Olivia Newton John, their music teacher, looks on with amazement.

CISSIE: When you started giggling during the Dying Swan 1 could have swooned with embarrassment

ADA Well that dancer was bandy and her feet were stuck out.

CISSIE: That posture is assumed to indicate that the bird is expiring.

ADA: Oh 1 could see that, she was sweating cobs. Here, what was that thing Nearenough was wearing round his bottom half.?

CISSIE: That was a codpiece.

ADA Biggest fish finger 1've ever seen.

ADA Looked more like a conger eel.

CISSIE: You really are pig ignorant, and now 1'm off to get changed because tonight, my Leonard and 1 are going to the opening of La Traviata.

ADA: You would'nt catch me eating that foreign muck

CISSIE: What on earth are you talking about?

ADA;   I'd sooner have a pan of broth....there's no taste in that Marconi

CISSIE: La Traviata is not an Italian restaurant, you fool it's an opera by Verdi....Oh 1 feel sorry for you, you'll never understand the deep emotional of a well performed aria.

ADA 1 I did when 1 was younger

CISSIE: To experience the thrill of Wagner's Loengrin.

ADA: Never bee that lucky...even during the war.

CISSIE: To be carried away by the sensuality of Borodin.

ADA: That's what 1 came over for...Borodin

CISSIE: What are you talking about?

ADA: I want to borodin some sugar and lard and let me have some Daz..

Cissie and Ada

Cissie: Well, we made it. Isn't it thrilling to be in London once more? We haven't been here since the end of the war. Do you remember those wonderful days, Ada? All those soldiers. Americans, free French and the Czechs.

Ada: I always got cash myself .

Cissie: Do you remember Big Al, the Australian marine?

Ada: Oo, yes, he fancied me. He once told me that when he saw me, time stood still. He said my face could stop a clock.

Cissie: He wasn't far wrong. To be honest, chuck, it was me he really desired. Did you know he asked me to go down under with him?

Ada: The mucky pup.

Cissie: He wanted me to see his beloved Antipodes.

Ada: I hope you kept your hands to yourself.

Cissie: He suffered with his feet, you know. All that marching through Burma, captured by the Japanese when he was cut off from his Chindits...

Ada: Fancy.

Cissie: Suffered with his feet. Did you ever see the size of his veruca?

Ada: No, but I didn't know him that well.

Cissie: That's why he limped. Because of his veruca. I used to try and ease it by rubbing it down with sandpaper. I nearly got it down to nothing.

Ada: What a waste.

Cissie: What are you talking about? Oh, you really are pig ignorant, Ada. You read sex into everything.

Ada: I wish you'd tell my Bert that. He might get the urge from the *Sporting Pink*. By the way, what are we going to see? Is it *Surprise Surprise* with that Celia Black?

Cissie: I wish it was, love, but it's *An Evening with Les Dawson*. I'm afraid the man on the door said he couldn't find enough people to sit through it.

Cissie and Ada

Cissie: [PUFFING] I've just been to WeightWatchers.

Ada: Were they closed?

Cissie: Don't be sarcastic, Ada, you're not exactly Twiggy's double, are you?

Les: Thank you very much. I'll have you know that I'm only twelve stone and some pounds.

Cissie: How many pounds?

Ada: Sixty-two.

Cissie: I can't understand it. I've been dieting for weeks. I should have lost some weight. My Leonard and I have been doing the 'F' Plan.

Ada: I know. I've seen your bedroom curtain drawn. Bert and I tried the 'F' once. Bert put his back out and I scraped my knees on the lino.

Cissie: Ada, you really are pig ignorant. The 'F' Plan is a diet. Not hanky panky. That's all you seem to think about. I blame it Bert. He's got sex on the brain.

Ada: I know, love, I just wish he'd lower it down and again. He hasn't per formed since Dunkirk. He says doing it makes the shrapnel move.

Cissie: You look washed out, Ada. You could do with a good holiday. Last year Leonard and I went to Greece.

Ada: Oh, Bert and I have been to Greece. We went on a Wallace Arnold Sunkissed Intercontinental holiday package tour on HP.

Cissie: Fancy. How did you get on with the food? Did you have the shish kebabs?

Ada: From the moment we arrived. Bert blamed it on the way they cooked the chips.

Cissie: I adore Athens. Did you see the Acropolis?

Ada: See it? We were never off it. Bert were so sore at the finish he wore a rubber ring on the coach back to Dover.

Cissie and Ada

Cissie: It would do you good to travel more, Ada. It would broaden you out.

Ada: If I get any broader I'll have to wear elastic knickers.

Cissie: No, I meant broaden your horizons. My Leonard and I are devotees of travel. Regular globe-trotters.

Ada: It'll be all that foreign food that does it. Too greasy for me. Get bunged up in Southport.

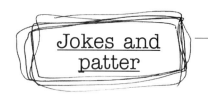

I said to the chemist,
'Can I have some sleeping pills for the wife?'
He said, 'Why?' I said, 'She keeps waking up.'

☆☆☆☆

There was an old maid from Genoa
And I blush when I think what Iowa
Now she's gone to her rest
And it's all for the best
Otherwise, I would borrow Samoa

☆☆☆☆

We had to get the doctor to look at Father eventually.
He diagnosed a severe attack of moth bites.
My dad said, 'Impossible.
We've a wardrobe full of moths there and I know
them all by their first names.'

☆☆☆☆

We were so poor at home I was brought up to believe
that tramps were conservative.

☆☆☆☆

I wouldn't say the room was small but the woodworm
were round-shouldered.

☆☆☆☆

The house was so dirty the mice suffered
from blackheads.

☆☆☆☆

I wouldn't say she was fat but she has so many chins shes uses a bookmark to find her mouth/necklace.

I wouldn't say the food was bad but Fanny Craddock was picketing the oven.

I was changing a tyre on my car the other day, and a fellow pulled up and opened my bonnet. I said, 'What the hell are you doing?' He said, 'If you're having the wheels I'm having the battery.'

Father was a keen trade unionist. He insisted on a tea break on his wedding night.

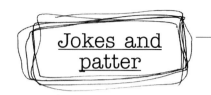

Jokes and patter

Descriptive patter

1 He displayed all the happiness of someone who's just won a month's holiday in Rotherham.

2 Her face was long and yellow with just a hint of fuzz on the lower chin. In fact it was like looking at an 'E'-type peach.

3 Her face had an expression on it that is usually associated with a female rhino having a breech delivery in a hammock.

4 When she smiled, it looked like a crack across a septic tank.

5 She possessed all the charm of a Tunisian culvert.

6 She looked about as happy as a stripper who's just found river sand in her G string.

7 The noise she made when she snored was akin to that made by a herd of Friesians breaking wind.

8 She was so fat, in case she fell down, the hospital fitted a towbar to her knickers.

9 I'm not saying I was an ugly baby, but as I was being born, the midwife took one look at me and shouted to my mother, 'For God's sake, bear up.'

They have loads of books on the market
on how to bring up your children.
I bought one called A *Hundred Ways to Stop
your Kid being Delinquent.*
I had the book five days before my kid destroyed it.
He knew 101 ways.

☆☆☆☆

I wouldn't say the show was lousy but business was so bad
we let one-eyed people in half price.

☆☆☆☆

But whatever I earn is going towards a worthy cause
and that is to send my wife and mother to the country...
India, Burma, Tibet... anywhere will do.

☆☆☆☆

I upset the wife's mother last Guy Fawkes night.
I fell off the fire.

☆☆☆☆

I wouldn't say the house was damp
but we didn't go into the cellar
for coal unless we wore shark repellant.

☆☆☆☆

Les was proud to be a member of the Water Rats – a charity that carries out splendid work for the theatre community and others. Even if he couldn't make a meeting, he always wrote a letter of apology – here are some extracts.

Les Dawson

DEAR SCRIBE RAT.

MY APOLOGIES FOR NOT BEING ABLE TO ATTEND LODGE THIS COMING SUNDAY, THE 15TH OF OCTOBER. I WOULD LIKE TO HAVE ATTENDED THE LADIES EVENING BUT UNFORTUNATELY TRAGEDY HAS STRUCK AT MY VERY FIBRE – LAST MONDAY EVENING AT 8·30 PM. THE ISRAELIS FOUND THE WIFE'S HIDING PLACE – IT WAS ONLY THREE YEARS AGO THAT I DISCOVERED SHE WAS A WAR CRIMINAL AND AN EX U. BOAT COMMANDER – SHE WAS DRUNK ONE AFTERNOON AND AS SHE LAY SLUMPED OVER HER MOTOR BIKE, I HEARD HER WHISTLING A SNATCH FROM THE "HORST WESSEL" OH I HAD BEEN SUSPICIOUS FOR SOME TIME– LITTLE THINGS BOTHERED ME SUCH AS A SWASTIKA PINNED TO HER TRUSS: THE WAY SHE'D STAND FOR HOURS BLOWING RASPBERRIES AT TERRITORIALS. ONE DAY I WAS CLEANING HER JACK BOOTS AND TRYING TO REMEMBER WHAT TERRY CANTOR HAD SAID ABOUT

Les during his year as King Rat with fellow Water Rat David Jason.

—

Les Dawson

Dear Scribe Rat,
I cannot attend Lodge this coming Sunday, because as you are no doubt aware, it is Stafford Cripps Week in Tunbridge Wells, and I have been asked to compere the Ointment Festival at the Carnival of Sauce Bands. It will be very nostalgic for me go back there, as in nineteen forty one I deserted from the Army Pay Corps, in the face of N.A.AF.I prices.
On a more serious note, older members of The Rats, will be saddened to hear that the Opera House Runcorn is being pulled down to make way for a sewage farm. This wonderful baroque theatre, which was opened in eighteen fiftyone by the Crown Prince of Neasden, was considered by many to be the last word in splendour. It was only a small theatre, in fact it was so small, the only panto they could put on was "Babes In The Tree"...Indeed on the opening night when the curtain went up so did the balcony.
I have in my possession, a play bill dated 2-5-9903 the top of the bill was the Dancing Narvick Duo and the masked banjos. Roscoe Chip, the American who blew omlettes through a dwarf's blouse was second spot, and Igor Fruit, the nude baritone (You may recall his bill matter..."Harmony with a hernia") was put on probation for relieving himself against a Hyde Park laburnum.
Edith Sopwith, the celebrated bassoonist, bruised an ear when a slater on the roof lost his balance and fell on her head as she was opening a pale ale with the rim of a cymbal. She married him in Rhyl but he turned out a rotter..he went from bad to

Les Dawson

Dear Scribe Rat.

I am unable to attend Lodge on the 21ST May owing to a television show in Newcastle on that date, the programme being a series called "Jokers Wild". Please convey my regards to all my fellow Rats and my regrets at being unable to be with them.

I have'nt recieved any voting papers in respect of Mr Lansdown (SORRY ABOUT THE "R" – I'M BLOODY IGNORANT) As a baby rat am I entitled to vote?

Water Rats

SAVOY-HOTEL — FUNCHAL — MADEIRA
SAVOY HOTEL — FUNCHAL — MADEIRA

BILHETE POSTAL

DEAR SCOUSE RAT
THE SUN BEATS DOWN
LIKE A SMILE FROM BERNARD DELFONT.
THE HOTEL IS SO BIG THE MICE
WEAR ST CHRISTOPHER MEDALS
AND YESTERDAY THE WIFE WAS
HARPOONED. IF THE CIGAR FUND
ISN'T CLAIMED PLEASE SEND
TO ME IN A STAMPED ADDRESSED
FILLET STEAK — PRICES HERE ARE
HIGHER THAN DAVID NIXON'S
WRINKLES _____ LOVE Les Dawson

TO

GRAND ORDER OF WATER RATS

PERESTRELLOS — PHOTOGRAPH

REPRODUÇÃO PROIBIDA

No. 43

Impresso na Noruega

Les Dawson

Dear Scribe Rat,

I cannot attend Lodge this coming Sunday
because I am busy filming "The Rita Webb Story"...
with Des O'Conner, who is playing the lead.
Its a good part that I have managed to get, I play
a Jewish call girl who opens Arab dustbins in the
heat of battle. Rock Hudson plays Lenin, and Jo Jac
and Johnny are the inside leg measurements.
If any Brother Rat wishes to spend a relaxing
vacation before his next spell of unemployment,
may I reccomend Spitz Hampton-On-The Crouch.
It lies north east of the island of Gurtyer in the
Outer Orkneys.
The beach stretches from the Sewage Reclaimation
Silos, to the ex war Department mine field.
On a clear day you can see the fog, and on one of the
early morning jaunts, one can often see crabs picking
their teeth clean of GREASE with a filtered nipper.
There is dancing twice a month on the jetty, and
some of the old fishermen still remember Ted Ray.
You can stay in the Hotel Splendide Del Mar..the
hotel is under a viaduct near a blouse factory, and
you are assured of a warm welcome indeed, mainly
because the chef is a fire bug. Nightlife abounds
aplenty...You can get a drink until half past seven
in Gladys Potts cafe, and the cabaret consists of
Roberto Cox and his Warsaw tambourine band..on
Tuesday evenings as an added bonus, a Dutch ventriloqui
-st, will answer any questions on goose farming and at
the same time oil his legs.

They hold a dinner dance in August in the sauna room
of the nearby Hemmoroid Clinic, so any artist can be

COCKK: "WHY DID THE CHICKEN CROSS THE ROAD"

FINGELBAUM: "THURSDAY"

COCKK: "YOU'VE HEARD IT BEFORE"

FINGELBAUM: "Lets lean against the river"....A One Two Three....(Organx
(Organ impression and Cockk blows suet up Fingel's kilt)

Needless to say the audiences were in an uproar at this oral riposte, which
which you can get off with a dry leather.So there you have it, at last a
written record of an act that once had Clifford Davies in stitches, they
hit him with Tony Hatch. Only Wee **Georgie** will recall the versatile duo
or perhaps Robert Orben who is George Martin's spiritual advisor.
A hastily penned note from Weinbeck Fingelbaum to a frump in aHuddersfield
bordello, tells the jade of his accident whilst clambering up the Xxxxxxxxx
Matterhorn on a Courtline excursion, it reads very movingly:

Dear Agnes,
AAAAAAAAAHHHHHHOOOOOOOO.

I hear that a cdrtain Peter Sellers is to made a Rat, l have no knowledge
of this gentleman, although l have heard he's a sort of Rxxxx Mike
Yarwood with money. Typical bloody ploy, he'll be Trap Guard in no time,
and here's me, a product of the more lowly aspects of show business, who
is destined never to hold office **because** of my colour and leanings to
Lesbianism. Do you think l enjoy being what l am? Did l ask God for a
webbed armpit? Do you for one moment imagine that l enjoy sexual emotion
at the sight of a hermit crab? No matter, you have your lives and l, well
l have a friend who **cle&ns** at a motorway washroom, I'll very fond of
Hunched Arthur, and he plays a recorder for a troupe of **mummers**...Time
for me to go out, looking always looking........

Rxxxxxxllyxxx Fraternally

LES DAWSON'S FUTURE ENGAGEMENTS

DECEMBER 8th   Rivington Pike Bed Wetting Institute and practise Briss.

December 14th   Dave Forester overcoat cleaning fund drive.

February 1st   Attack agent.

RECIPE: HALIFAX BRAISED MOLE.

PART ONE: "THE INGREDIENTS"

ONE MOLE, ELDERLY, MALE IF POSSIBLE. BAG OF ICED BARLEY. FOUR EGGS AND TWO
MONGOOSE BALLS. OUNCE OF BURNT PITCH WITH NUTMEG. THREE IRONED SKIN GRAFTS
Next week: "Preparation"

Another regular character in the 1970s, Happy Harry often caused confusion.

Happy Harry

Harry: Are you the manager, my good man?

Colin: I am indeed. What is the problem?

Harry: It's about the window cleaner on the fourteenth floor...

Colin: How dare you suggest that old George, our paragon of toil, has in any way caused offence! You grotesque imbecile, you ill-dressed muckraker. In all the years he has been with us, not one whisper of scandal has ever been in evidence. And another thing, you uncouth moron, I've seen your wife, she's bovine, do you hear? As nondescript as your ill-kempt self. Now before I order you out, what did your odious paramour say?

Harry: He's fell off.

Happy Harry

Harry: Nice place you've got 'ere. Tell me, young man, how much is that refrigerator over there, the big'un?

Colin: Out of your reach I'm afraid, that fridge is £300, but freezes to an absolute zero.

Harry: Eeh, very good but, mind you, I've got one similar to that one and I have summat in it that keeps hot.

Colin: Why you dolt, you addle-pated dullard, the very purpose of refrigeration is to freeze produce and those expensive models over there are the finest ones of their kind and you, you half-wit, you alcoholically-vertiginous northern clod have the audacity to come in this high class store and mouth drivel. What on earth can possibly stay hot in your fridge?

Harry: Mustard.

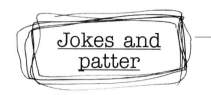

These quick sketches include one with John Cleese, who was a regular on Sez Les in the early 1970s.

Quickie Runners

Les: Play it again, Sam.
John Cleese: Certainly not.

Les (as nun): The hills are alive!
John: Don't be so absurd.

Les: I did it my way!
John: Yes, and you botched it.

☆☆☆☆

All the mother-in-law talks about is how mean her husband is. When he found out he was going bald, rather than buy a wig, he changed his religion so he could wear a turban. I wouldn't say he's that mean, although he does keep an old-fashioned mangle out the back yard to get the last kick from his toothpaste tubes.

☆☆☆☆

I danced the polka with a typical German fraulein. She was the spitting image of Goering. The band played all the old German songs like 'Annie get Your Luger' and a wartime song about paratroops from the Rhine Valley invading the town of Minehead. You probably know it, it was called 'Rhine Troops are Falling on Minehead'.

☆☆☆☆

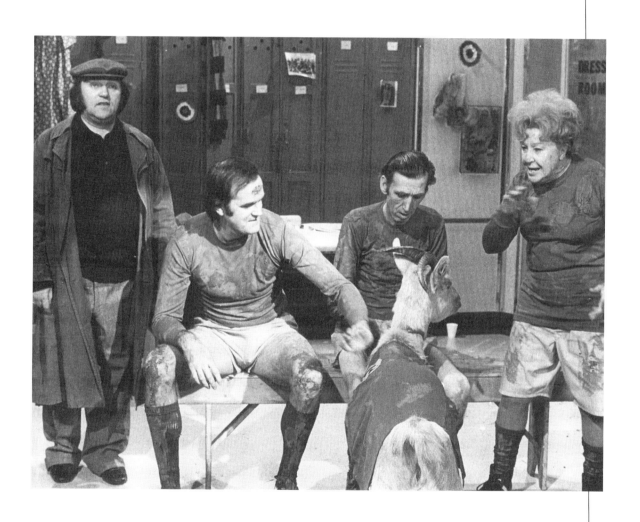

One of Les's hilarious sketches, featuring John Cleese, Eli Wood and Noel Gordon.

I was in Scotland and I found a restaurant that did unusual dishes. The favourite was noses of whelks in butter. Unfortunately they were long-nosed whelks which were hard to get because that particular species only mated once a year down a drain in Swanley.

They also served jugged hare in marmalade, but again that was a very rare dish. You could get roast wren, but it's only a little bird and you would still be hungry after having one. The main dish was whale meat on toast, but that was a bit greasy.

I went in one day and I asked for buttered noses of whelks. They had none, no hare, just wren and, of course, whale meat. I said, 'Haven't you got anything else?' And the owner looked at me and sang:

'Whale meat again, got roast wren, got no hare. Butter-nosed whelks, mate, again down Swanley drain.'

○ ○○○

I went into a restaurant of high repute and the cuisine was a veritable tone poem to the art gastronomic. I summoned the head waiter and bade him send my respects to the chef.

'The culinary expertise was a positive Valhalla of taste and aroma,' I intoned gravely. 'The poulette d'Anglais was a dish about which to make eulogies and the swan liver pate and goose vol au vent a la Sicile were sonnets to the nymphs of Olympia.'

The waiter said, 'It is we who should thank you, sir. It is very rare that we are privileged to have a gourmet of your calibre in here.'

I said, 'That's very nice of you to say so, but I had intended never to dine here again after my last experience when you yourself, bodily and somewhat brutally, threw me out because I couldn't pay for the meal.'

The waiter paled and croaked, 'Please forgive me, sir, it was obviously a grave error of judgement.'

'Not at all. In fact, I'll have to trouble you again.'

53

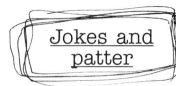

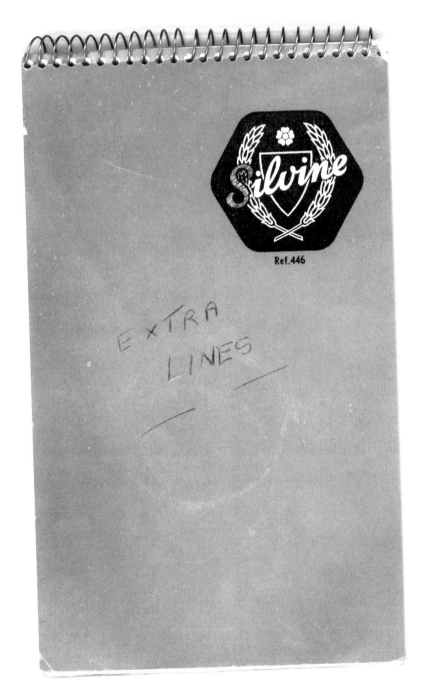

Silvine

Ref.446

EXTRA
LINES

She told me it was her 30th birthday.
So I put thirty candles on her cake,
arranged in the shape of a question mark.

Duck goes in the chemist's shop.
'A tube of lipsol please.'
'Certainly, that will be fifty pence.'
'Put it on my bill, please'

My wife is ignorant –
no idea of anything, especially music.
She thought Bizet's *Carmen* was a Spanish bus driver.

I wouldn't say the house was damp but the woodworm
breathed through straws.

I wouldn't say the plane was old but we were hijacked
by the Wright brothers.

They say you should always smile when you're poor.
It's perfectly true. They've just rushed the wife to hospital,
delirious with laughter.

It took Les years of struggle to get recognition, but once he had, he was in demand not only for his regular series but also as a special guest – so more gags needed to be created.

Les Dawson special

Show one

[SING: 'MY WAY']

When the going gets rough and life's vicissitudes churn your dreams into a positive maelstrom of despair, do not lose heart. In the words of that ballad, do you what you believe is right and do it your way.

Some two years ago I went through such a period of desolation. Nothing went the way I wanted it to. My career was going downhill faster than a rabbit with a promise. I was dying so often I got tape measures from undertakers. I couldn't raise a laugh anywhere. I played one theatre and the silence I endured through my act was so intense that the mere shifting of a cough lozenge from one molar to another reverberated like a musket volley. I couldn't pay the rent, I kept getting evicted. In fact, my furniture was thrown onto the streets so often I had the loose covers made to match the pavements.

I was about to mug a baby for his rusk when I spotted a light shimmering through the broken stained-glass window of a decrepit chapel. I entered and saw kneeling by the altar an old man whose care-worn face was etched with lines of despair and anxiety. I put my arm around his thing shoulders and whispered, 'What is it, old fellow?' He looked at me with watery eyes and croaked, 'It's the wife. She's up there.' He pointed heavenwards. Suddenly my troubles seemed so small compared to his grief. I said in a choked voice, 'Don't worry, she's out of it all now, she's with the angels.' He said, 'She isn't, she's pinching lead off the roof.'

Les and Shirley Bassey perform 'A Couple of Swells' on her show.

LES DAWSON

... FULL CABARET ACT.....LES DAWSON...

*I wandered thro' a valley of timeless serenity...etc.
                    tag: "HORSEMUCK"

There was a time in the early days of the music hall when certain comedian
would walk on the stage wearing a red nose and blowing raspberries at the
audience, they were of course, third rate inferior performers who were
destinied for theatrical obscurity, tonight in an effort to prove that my
act is incredibly versatile and intellectual as well as boring, 1 would
like to play for you upon the pianoforte, not one but two pieces, the
first is an adaptation from a work by Mozart entitled:"In an 18th
century drawing room, swiftly followed by the theme from that much
publisised movie..."Love Story"....thank you. (Play and then...Rasp)

I've often heard it said that sometimes when a comedian walks onto a
stage, he takes one look at the audience and gets so frightened by the
indifference he sees on their faces, that he just xxxx stands there
wishing that the entire night was over so that he can creep outx like a
cat that's missed the ashes...I had a good peep throught the makeshift
curtains before 1 came on and all 1 can say is: Good Evening, welcome
to the show and....(National Anthem)

Its a grrat pleasure to be appearing here tonight in this superbly
furnished...(Whatever) ...before such a wonderful audience, wonderful
musicians in this wonderful township of........And thats one thing
you'll find about me 1 maybe a lousy comic but 1'm the biggest creep in
the business....I must say 1've always had a soft spot for......its
a swamp, but 1 love coming to this club its got a wonderful atmosphere,
it reminds me of home, its filthy and full of strangers...and when 1
arrived this morning the management could'nt do enough for me so they
did'nt bother...the staff here are nice they treat each other like
brothers...the Kray Brothers...xxxdxxhxyxxvxxgxxxxxxxxxxxxgxx And you should
see the dressing room they've given me...well somebody should especially
a health inspector...its got a carpet down God knows when it was last
vaacummed but the beetles walk across it on stilts...Its right at the top
of the building, 1 don't know how high it is but my xxxxx coat hanger's
full of falcon droppings...you even get a nose bleed off the wood worm.
But there is one thing you can be proud of here and that is the superb
orchestra you've got each and evey one of these musicians is a marvellous
individual insrtumentalist...its only when they play together its such
a bloody row...

The Queen's Silver Jubilee Show

Night of a Hundred Stars

But nothing can mar my delight at actually appearing on the stage of the National Theatre. The National Theatre – a sort of Festival Hall with overdrafts. A superb example of baroque Wimpey.

When my agent phoned me about this engagement it came as a shock because the way the work's coming in I thought he'd gone down with the *Titanic*. On winged feet I sped round to the office – where he cleans – and there he was, on his knees, in front of a Brenard Delfont cigar butt. As he gave me the contract to sign I could tell he was excited. His hands were shaking so much he damn near dropped his ready reckoner. I could understand his excitement. After all, my world is vastly removed from that of the legitimate theatre, of Shakespeare and Ibsen. Let's face it, in some of the places I play, the audience think *Timon of Athens* is one of the Muppets.

Les in panto with John Nettles.

This popular illusionist and TV host was a regular target – and bald!

The David Nixon Show

Thames TV, programme 6

David: I don't know about you ladies and gentlemen, but I can't stand comedians who come onto a show and start off by saying, 'A funny thing happened to me on the way to the theatre tonight.' Invariably, the ones who do so are boring and destined for obscurity. That's why it's a pleasure to introduce my next guest... A man who has put culture and humour and intellectualism into variety. Ladies and gentlemen – Les Dawson.

[PLAY]

Les: A funny thing happened to me on the way to the theatre tonight. I'm sorry about that and you might find it hard to believe but I studied the piano under Gladys Mills – mind you, I had to give it up. I kept getting my fingers caught in her garters. I've upset David Nixon. He's in a hell of a temper now – he's stood in a corner gnashing his teeth and pulling someone else's hair out. I wanted to please him because I need the money badly – in fact to give you some idea how desperate things are financially with my family, we're still trying to live up to the Joneses next door and they're under the care of Oxfam. It's ridiculous. The mice in our kitchen are setting traps for us.

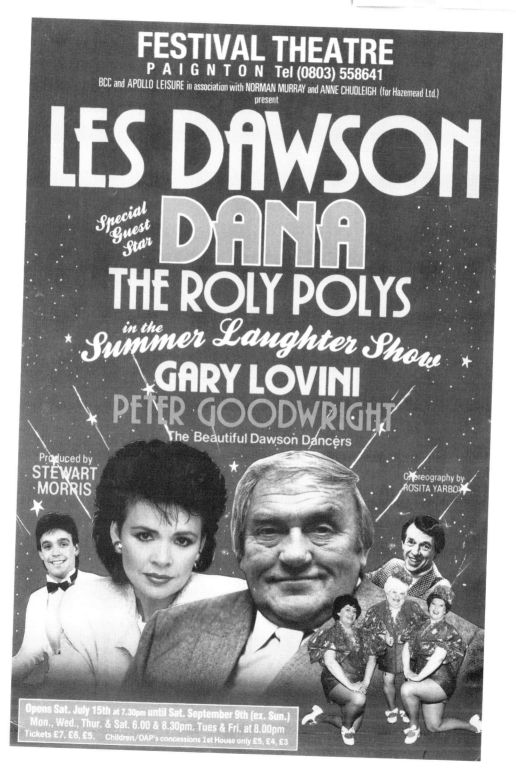

FESTIVAL THEATRE
PAIGNTON Tel (0803) 558641
BCC and APOLLO LEISURE in association with NORMAN MURRAY and ANNE CHUDLEIGH (for Hazemead Ltd.)
present

LES DAWSON

Special Guest Star **DANA**

THE ROLY POLYS

in the *Summer Laughter Show*

GARY LOVINI
PETER GOODWRIGHT
The Beautiful Dawson Dancers

Produced by
STEWART MORRIS

Choreography by
ROSITA YARBOY

Opens Sat. July 15th at 7.30pm until Sat. September 9th (ex. Sun.)
Mon., Wed., Thur. & Sat. 6.00 & 8.30pm. Tues & Fri. at 8.00pm
Tickets £7, £6, £5.   Children/OAP's concessions 1st House only £5, £4, £3

61

Show Eight

I was born in a small village, infact it was so small we took it in
when it rained...It was a poor village in in fact the wishing well
was full of I.o.u's....The village was miles off the beaten track ...
so remote, Dr acula got in for the Liberals. We were famous for one thing
a red indian who sat on a high crag wrapped in his blanket, he'd been
there ever since anyone could remember and he was consulted by farmers
and people alike becaude he could predict the weather better than any
satellite.People would say what will it be like tomorrow? He'd put his
hea d under his blanket and mumble Oha ha...Then he straighten up
and say tomorrow fine but rain later. rrom all over the world people
would come to hear him predict from within his magic blanket...1 went
back to the village recently after many years and he was till there
1 said how, can your magic blanket tell me what the weather will be
like at the week end...He dived under his blanket came out and shook his
head me no tell, 1 said dont tell me your magic has gone...he said no
my wireless broke......xjxix Whatever the weather it's xixxxxxxxxx
a lways sunny on Blankety Bkank, the show that makes you want to get up
xxix go to bingo

Christmas stand up spot

If someone doesn't come up an' change my nappy soon, they'll be having lifeboat drill in this cot. Talk about feeling damp: it won't be long before there's a rainbow round my neck. What a flaming way to spend the festive season, bunged up here with a dummy full of jam and a plastic Hong Kong rattle. Just look at it – where the hell's the pleasure in shaking that? I'm stood here like Mothercare's answer to Edmundo Ross. Oh, come on somebody, in another half hour they'll have built a damp course in my romper suit.

I thought Christmas was a time when kids were supposed to enjoy themselves. But you can't have any fun with grown-ups. They do their best to get you to walk and talk and as soon as you do, they tell you to sit down and shut up. For Christmas dinner they had turkey, mince pies and pudding. All I got was a lukewarm bottle full of lumpy milk. Didn't enjoy it – one good suck and the teat's clogged up. That's bad enough, but after you've finally gagged the revolting mess down, somebody throws you over their shoulder and knocks seven bells out of you.

Shows & specials

The Good Old Days

Thank you for that applause. You have impeccable taste. However, the warmth of your welcome has put me in a retrospective mood... a little sombre music please – thank you. Our resident orchestra, ladies and gentlemen, who quite often play 'til the cows come home – and by the sound of the violin, they've arrived.

Many of you will remember the television saga entitled *Roots*. It was a sort of *Crossroads* with spears. As I watched each episode, a burning desire emerged to learn something of my own heritage, to discover the roots of the Dawson family tree. This desire was fanned into a raging fire following a peculiar incident at Horsebottom Towers near the Wigan motorway urinal maintenance depot.

This old stately house is the seat of the Potts Belching family, who founded the first geriatric sex shop. While bending over the rim of a pit where Cromwell used to bait lapsed Jesuits, a partly-bald goat sank his decaying molars into my fully exposed posterior. Not unnaturally, I leapt into the air like a frustrated kangaroo that's just had a promise and landed on top of a heap of dried sheep dung. The seat of my trousers was agape and my naked rump peeped out, a sight which I was later assured was rather like a bruised peach under a pelmet.

From behind a tuft of groundsel, an elderly toothless man appeared and commenced to laugh in a series of hoarse asthmatic wheezes. I was about to admonish the churl when his gaze became riveted on a birthmark that I am cursed with on my left thigh. It's an odd blemish, a sort of cross between a strawberry and a duck's foot. Upon seeing it the old loon went on his knees, kissed the hem of my braces and shouted in ringing tones: 'You've come home, Sir Guy...'

..."LES DAWSON AND FRIENDS"...SHOW TWO

SING: "THERE'S A PLACE FOR US"

"Yes ladies and gentlemen, as the words of that song suggest, ~~fanx~~ For all of us there is a place...and that place is for the majority of people. a home of one's own...A material dream to build on: A nest in which to raise a family: A beckoning refuge in a world so often raddled with hostility...Like so many other married couples, when the wife and l were first wed, we could·nt afford a place of our own, so we had to live with her parents...and do n·t for moment think it was·nt enjoyable... because it was·nt...l did·nt see eye to eye with the mother-in-law, which is·nt surprising because she's six foot four...They wrote a television series about my relationship with the wife's mother, you may remember it it was called "Mission Impossible!"...From the moment we stayed there, she never stopped talking and having a go at me...l·ve only got one decent photograph of her, it must have been taken with a hi-speed camera because its the only one of her where her mouth's shut...She never sat down, she was on the go so often she had a fan belt on her drawers... She played hell if l touched anything, she·d shake me like a bag of lentils and shout:"Don·t dare put the television on, its mine and paid for, I·ll select the programmes and switch it on...not you, and another thing don't use the immersion heater unless l get two days notice , and l'll put it on...Don't leave a ring in the bath and don't ever put your dirty feet on my uncut mocequette...On night she went to the cinema l phoned up and they flashed a message on the screen telling her to come home...she shot back faster than a recently doctored ferret, stood in thelounge panting like a station horse at the knackers..."what's wrong" she screamed..."~~Natkixgx~~ l said nothing...the fire wants poking...

One of Les's proudest moments, being introduced to Her Majesty.

The Royal Command Performance

For those of you in the audience who have never attended this magnificent spectacle before, it must be a great thrill to be here tonight under the same roof and seeing in person for the first time... a Northern comic. You've heard of the North of England – that's the bit that lies beyond the listening posts at Watford. People often ask me, 'Is there any difference in the humour between the North and the South?' Well, I've never found any. They don't laugh at me up there either. There are one or two basic difference however. In the North we still brew beer that makes you tipsy. Down here if you drink too much it gives you the bends. In the North, husbands still wear the trousers – you can see them under their aprons. In Lancashire, we still have the common sense to boil a black pudding. Down here you fry them until they lie on the plate like something out of *Quatermass*.

Windsor Charity for Prince Phillip

Opening to be fixed

It's difficult to describe the wife's mother, but she's a sort of Judge Jeffreys with knickers. She sails through life like a badly-chipped frigate and her favourite meal is piranha fish fingers. She's never forgiven me for marrying her only daughter. On our wedding day she cried all through the ceremony. She had her hand fast in the collection box. Three months ago she came to live with us. As soon as I heard the knock on the door I knew it was her because the mice were throwing themselves on the traps. And our budgie was advertising for a beak rivetter.

[INTO 'LOVE STORY']

End: If ever in the North of England where I live and you are near my home, please call in, the front door's always open. We can't shut the damn thing.

<u>Seaside Special, Great Yarmouth</u>

Saturday 18 June, 1977

A philosopher once said that applause is music to an artist's ears. If it's
true then all I can say in response to the clap you gave me is, 'Good
evening, welcome to the show and... "Colonel Bogey".'

Welcome to *Seaside Special* which, because of the need for economy, is
coming from inside this hastily-erected, cut-price, Zeppelin heat-shield.
Marvellous, isn't it, every show I've done for the BBC this jubilee year
has been from a ruddy tent. I must be the only man in the country who
suffers from hay fever and guy-rope rash. Work for the BBC, they said,
you can be sure of support from them. I got support all right – Billy Cotton
sold me a truss.

Nothing's gone well at all today. Coming here I got stuck in a traffic jam
at ... I don't know how long it had been there, but there was a car in front
with a sign saying 'Just married' and there was three kids in the back.

I'm not happy about the hotel they've put me in. For a start, it's in a
rough area of the town. Well, you can tell how tough it is, I got mugged
last night by a nun. You've never seen a house like it... it's decorated in
early Gestapo.

I saw a photograph of Raquel Welch in a topless dress the other day. It
was like looking at Lord Longford and David Nixon butting one another.
Mind you, being bald has it's problems for David. Every time he goes to a
bowling alley, people put their fingers up his nose.

Summertime Special Eastbourne

Opening

Our next star guest was for many years a stand-in on
Emmerdale Farm, but he gave it up when he realised
what he was standing in. He's just returned from a tour
of haemorrhoid clinics where he received a standing
ovation. Ladies and gentlemen, Roger Kitter.

Les switching on the Blackpool illuminations in 1986.

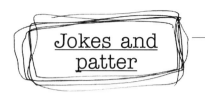

I wouldn't say the room was small but the toaster lay on its side.

☆☆☆☆

And they expect us to teach our kids the facts of life. I finally plucked up courage and told my son about the birds and bees. When I'd finished I said, 'Well, son, you heard what I told you. Now what do you say? He said, 'Not bad, Dad, you got most of it right.'

☆☆☆☆

I wouldn't say the room was small but you had to soak your dentures in shifts.

☆☆☆☆

I wouldn't say the house was damp but the goldfish climbed out of the bowl to breath.

☆☆☆☆

I wouldn't say she was ignorant but she wondered if Black Power was cheaper than gas.

Les would rework gags and here is one with an alternative ending from a later revision.

And one night, from the gin-soaked lips of a pockmarked Lascar who was in the arms of a frump in a Huddersfield bordello, came the words that put me on the right path to understanding. He said: 'Seek ye the truth in Tibet.'

And so I signed on as a ship's carpenter. It was a nightmare voyage – storms, disease and mutiny – but at last we reached Knutsford. I hated the trip. The ship was so old they started it with a whip and the rats wore powdered wigs. At last we docked in the torrid hell of Kowloon and I donned the saffron robes of the Buddhists and trekked to the peaks of Nepal.

In the reeking horror of a Kathmandu bingo hall, an old crone with a full house told me of a monastery where I would find the old wise one who knew the secret of a happy life. And so, armed with a bag of Patna rice, a bottle of chutney and some watercress sandwiches, I began to scale the brooding Hymalayas. My fingers were torn and bleeding as I scrabbled to the summit. The wind tore holes in my vest and trilby and near the Indian border I got frostbite up the Khyber... My lips were like iced frankfurters and my eyelashes were knitted with snow.

Eventually, I reached the bleak outline of the monastery and two monks dragged me inside the echoing stone chamber and laid me on a dirty straw mat that hadn't got a single flea in it – they were all married with families.

Finally, I had an audience with the old wise man. I knelt before him in the flickering light of guttering candles and I said, 'Tell me, oh wise one, what is the secret of a happy life?' And he said softly, with his thin hands like autumn leaves playing with his prayer wheel, 'The secret of life, my son, is have no enemies, only friends. I am over 200 years old and I have no enemies.' 'How did you manage to live for so long without any?' I asked. He looked at me and whispered, 'I shot the bloody lot.'

○ ○ ○ ○

It was terrible – the ship was so old, the rats wore powdered wigs and the captain still had nightmares about the Armada. I jumped ship at Kowloon and trekked to Tibet, dressed in saffron robes and holding a begging bowl. As I climbed the Himalayas, my eyelids were caked with snot, my lips were scarred with the buffeting winds and I got frostbite up the Khyber... At last I reached my goal, for there squatting on a ledge, his face hidden in a dark cowl, was the Old Wise One. As the mist swirled around us and the wind yawned a lament, I said to the Old Wise One, 'Help me, I who travelled far. What is the meaning of life?' He looked at me and croaked, 'I am over 200 years old, my son, and for a hundred of them I have sat here on this damp stone ledge.' 'Old man,' I whispered reverently, 'What have you got from it all?' And he looked at me and he said softly, 'Piles.'

Radio days

Even though Les is best known for his TV work, he also did lots of radio work and came up with ideas for his own radio programmes or future ones.

<u>Radio series commencing 6 April</u>

<u>Show two</u>

I got into conversation with a man who claimed to have trained the great boxer Jack Dempsey. It appears that he hated Gene Tunney because Tunney had two unusual pets: a giant hare and a panda that did an impression of a donkey. Dempsey taunted Tunney by saying he could beat him wearing a woman's dress, a maxi-dress and he was also going to batter Tunney's hare with a minced piece of steak. Dempsey hired a band and every night he would stand outside Tunney's house and sing:

'I'll be gowned to beat you in a maxi Tunney batter, the hare about a half-mashed steak, so Tunney don't be late, I want to be there when your panda's braying'.

<u>BBC radio show</u>

April, Manchester

<u>Closing spot</u>

I hope you all enjoy the sound of our big orchestra playing such wonderful music and when you hear the melodies, one is grateful for those great song writers who gave us so many unforgettable tunes – George and Ira Gershwin, Rodgers and Hart, Lerner and Loewe, Gilbert and Sullivan and then, later again, the team of Rodgers and Hammerstein.

Tonight I would like to pay tribute to the musical talents of that celebrated couple from Lancashire, Arkwright and Catchpole. They should have been the most famous song-writing team in the world, but fate saw fit to burden them with problems.

Len Arkwright, for instance, had no sense of direction, which explains why he wrote such musical shows as *North Pacific* and *East Side Story*. His songs were the same. 'I left my throat in Sutton Coldfield'and my favourite, 'West of the Border up Mexico Way'.

His partner, Ernie Catchpole, was colour blind. He wrote many songs: 'I'm Dreaming of a Brown Christmas', 'I Want some Puce Roses for a Green Lady' and few will have forgotten his masterpiece, 'Beige Sails in the Sunset'.

THE DAWSON SHOW BBC radio

13 July

Those drums, gad how they bring back memories... It's years since I was in Bradford.

As a child, I was so ugly, Mothercare put shutters on my pram. Mine hasn't been an easy life – I am the last of the big game hunters. The natives call us bwanas. And there's not many of us left. In Africa today you can hear them sing: 'Yes, we have no bwanas.'

It's my job to catch animals for rich people, shoot them, stuff them and have them mounted or, if they prefer, just shaking hands. To be a big game hunter, you've got to be tough. Last week I broke a six-inch plank with my head and, just like that, concussion.

You've also got to sleep in the open air and generally rough it. For years all I had was an old sleeping bag but, thank God, she went back to her mother. What a woman, she was so fat, every time she hung her bra on the line to dry, a camel made love to it.

Making a fire in the jungle can be tricky. If you're matches are damp, it's either the start of the monsoon rains that did it or you've got a cat in your haversack. The best thing to do if that happens is to join the Boy Scouts and rub Ralph Reader's legs together. Food is often a problem when you're out on safari. Sometimes you may be lucky and stumble across a snake or a worn-out pygmy – and let's face it, there's nothing more delicious than a snake and pygmy pie. The normal food is beans, haricot beans, soya beans, runner beans and the answer, my friend, is blowing in the wind.

On average I get on well with the native tribesmen. I played cards with some of them last week, the wife said, 'Zulus?' I said, 'No, I won two quid.'

Some natives are hostile. A three-foot native from the Hoo Hoo Tribe – they're called the Hoo Hoo Tribe because they run through long grass with their trousers off – once came up behind me and snarled, 'Stick 'em up – this isn't a banana in your back.' I said, 'In that case you'd better stand on a chair, 'cos you're not in my back.' He took everything, clothing the lot and left the wife and I naked on a mountain pass with the wind blowing round our visas.

I turned to the wife, she was shoving snuff up her nose with a snooker cue. I said, 'He's taken everything, my beloved. She said, 'Oh no he hasn't. I managed to save the holiday money, the camera and the passports by hiding them in my mouth.' I said, 'It's a pity your mother wasn't with us then we could have saved the suitcases.'

Some people are scared of animals, particularly the aardvark, but that's nonsense because aardvark never killed anybody. Catching bears can be tricky but if you happen to be in the Arctic, you'll find that polar bears love marrowfat peas. All you do is cut a hole in the ice, scatter the peas around it and when the bear comes down for a pea, just kick it in the icehole.

Listen to Les BBC radio show

June series

[MUSIC: 'AULD LANG SYNE']

He bought a watch that was shock-proof, water-proof and cost £200. He'd only had it a day and it blew up. He bought a suit with two pair of pants and burnt a hole in the jacket. He married a woman who told him she had six kids all in the cemetary. It wasn't until after the wedding she told him they were only playing there. His wife was also very unlucky. One day a pixie popped up from a well in Cornwall and gave her a fairy medal on a chain and she never had another day's bad luck – that night as she went home on her bike, the medal got caught in the spokes and the chain strangled her. I once gave him a pair of shoes that were too tight for him but he insisted on wearing them. I said, 'But why? They're far too small for you.' He said, 'Listen, the only pleasure I get is taking the bloody things off.'

LES DAWSON

DRESSED ONLY IN INVERNESS CAPE - GANNET SPATS AND THIGH BOOTS

LES: ~~THEY They~~ **SHE** took Ivor in and treated him like ~~their~~ **HER** own child, and ~~re~~-named him Ivor Datsun, he soon got fed up with that because people kept following him about and asking him for spares. **SO HE RAN AWAY.** ~~Finaly Xxxxxxxxxtakexxxxxxxxxxfxitx and two months later after a stranded motorist had asked him to grab his distributer, Ivor ran away.~~

ROY: He got a job with a plastic surgeon, it was Ivor's job to ~~cut~~ **SNIP OFF** the ends of big noses, the wages were poor but the tips were enormous...He became very good at it ~~and~~ so much so, a Rabbi offered him the job as his assistant....

LES: But he turned it down because it was a different religion and he was'nt cut out for it.

JULIAN: He undertook many types of employment, for a time he kept racing pidgeons, but that did'nt last long, it was'nt the upkeep so much it was the overheads he had to watch

LES: ~~The fate took a hand~~ Then Fate took a hand, a wealthy Bengal curry maker, heard of Ivor's exploration of Pontin's, and offered him a years supply of dill pickle, if Ivor Longbottom could find the quickest way to send frozen chapattis up to Carlisle...It was spur he needed.

ROY: With a small party of native bearers from Clapham, he ~~setxxxxx~~ set off on his historic journey, his diary records the full adventure.

JULIAN: April the 1st....Camped on the hard shoulder near Watford, weather cold 1 sleep under the stars with only a flea bitten sleeping bag..but she's going home tomorrow.

~~LESxxAprilx2ndxxThankxGodxthexsleepingxbagxxxgonexhomextoxherxmotherxx~~

LES: April 3rd. Saw an astonishing sight, one of my native bearers on a tandem passed a Rolls Royce going at a 100 miles an hour...apparently his braces were caught on the bumpers

FOOD RUNNING OUT - LIVING ON FINCH MEAT AND CHIMPANZEE KNUCKLE BONES

ROY: April 6th, Reached Rotherham, ~~ItxxxxxxxxxxxxxxxIeftxxxxxxxxxonly~~ *IT WAS CLOSED* ~~xxmpanionxisxxxderangedxxtrafficxwardenxwhoxxxjustxhadxthexworldxtxxx cheapestxbrainxoperationxxitxonlyxcostxfourpencexxxndx~~ Weather bad now, ~~There was a float but~~ managed to ~~exchange~~ talk a curious native ~~in a pre war Austin to exchange a pie and mushy peas for a bingo card.~~

JULIAN: ~~Strxxxxx~~ Strange markings on a stick, reads A.A. is this a warning Bearers fled this day the 7th, 18m all alone but kept my sanity by juggling with a ton of loose soot.

LES: 9th April, 1 reach Leeds in torrential rain, the natives here ~~speakxxmxxxpeculiarxxxxx~~ speak in a peculiar dialect, as 1 tottered up the M.I. ~~xxxxx~~

If you can't laugh at your troubles then laugh at his, as you *Listen to Les.*

[WITH ORCHESTA: 'PUT ON A HAPPY FACE']

   Thank you – well met fellow humans for that munificent approbation. Dawson's disseration today is an essay titled 'The Holiday'.
   I boarded the grime-smeared and vandalised charabanc with some trepidation, because it was quite apparent that the motor coach had seen better days. In fact, by the look of it, it had more than likely transported Hannibal across the Alps – it really was a sorry sight to behold. It was, for a start, so old that the driver admitted that it didn't run on petrol, it went along on a mixture of swamp gas and bad droppings and the mudguards were thatched.
   Further investigation into the bowels of the engine revealed that it didn't possess a fan belt, just a length of elastic from Joan of Arc's knickers. The driver, a gap-toothed Latvian with a wooden foot, confessed that it was too old to be serviced anymore, so twice a year they took it to Lourdes. We filed aboard the coach and the driver held a raffle and the winner got a seat.

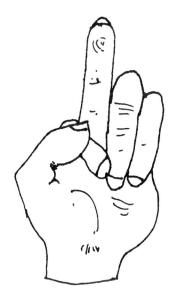

If you can't laugh at your troubles, then laugh at his as you *Listen to Les*.

[MUSIC]

Within the dark confines of the neglected burial ground, the naked branches of the decaying trees clawed at the sullen sky like the fingers of an abandoned harlot. The ashen-faced mourners hunched together closer as the cold grey fog embraced them in its clammy shroud, the wind howled like a lost soul in dire torment and behind the dark, brooding, rain-sodden hills a demented dwarf strangled his pet raccoon. As the first sods of rancid earth fell upon the coffin lid, a small elderly man groaned aloud as if in descant to the drone of the priest's lament.

I whispered to him, 'Was the deceased a relative, sir?' He nodded and croaked, 'Yes, my wife.My third wife in actual fact.' 'My sincere condolences, tragedy has indeed dogged your footsteps', I said with pity cloying my words. He looked at me and replied, 'My first wife died from eating mushrooms in Burma. I returned home and remarried and five years later my second wife passed away as a result of eating poisoned mushrooms. I married yet again and my third wife died from strangulation.' I paled and put my arm around the shoulder of the sorrowing man. 'How did it happen?' He said, 'She wouldn't eat the ruddy mushrooms'.

Listen to Les

<u>Radio show opening</u>

Good evening... and welcome to *Listen to Les*, the radio show that is as popular with the public as an advert for the pill is in Mothercare. In technical wireless terms, this show is known as: Collected Reminiscences and Auricular Paraphernalia or, to use the abbreviation as many do, CRAAP.

It's a great pleasure to be appearing here tonight in this thinly disguised conduit warehouse. Our producer, Jim Casey, is a wonderful man. I'm not saying he's a heavy drinker, but he was late for work yesterday and vodka shares slumped. He's given me a lovely dressing room, one of the latest type – you don't have a key to get in, just a penny.

We hope to bring you some unusual items in this programme. On the bill tonight we have a dwarf from Wigan who can juggle with a tub of loose soot and a vicar's wife who does a strip-tease in a bucket of ferrets. She's a very hard-bitten woman who used to lead a strike picket outside a chicken pox vaccine factory where she caught the disease. It's the first time in history that a picket's been pocked.

Tonight we'll be paying tribute to Quentin McGripknickers, the Scottish man who was dropped behind enemy lines during the last war with a length of rubber tube and some radishes. The idea was to put the wind up Hitler. He was capatured by the Gestapo and tortured in the most fiendish manner – they nailed his feet to a plank and played a Jimmy Shand record.

And as a surprise guest, ladies and gentlemen, we have in the audience here tonight a man who has done so much for British boxing – a big hand please for Mr Henry Cooper. Sorry, missus.

If you can't laugh at your troubles, then laugh at his, as you *Listen to Les*.

[PLAY 'PUT ON A HAPPY FACE]

The news that Agatha Louise, the wife's eldest sister, was to be married came as something of an emotional tremor, because the lady in question had been on the shelf so long she looked like a jar of preserves. In the past, poor lass, she had been frequently jilted. In fact, she had been kept waiting at the church so often the vicar made her wear a parking meter. Frankly, it wasn't surprising, because physically she is far from attractive. For instance, she is so thin, when she wears a fur coat she looks rather like a discarded strip of lagging from a kitchen waste pipe. Some two years ago she went for an X-ray and the doctor had to bend her double to get a picture. Her eyes are pits of malice, with the sort of frustration in them that one sees in a hedgehog that discovers it's mating with a yard brush. I first met her at a family funeral wearing a thick black veil. When she raised it she was arrested for indecent exposure.

Her two bridesmaids were large ladies, who would no doubt have been an asset as prop forwards for Wigan. Both were muscular and one had a faint moustache and a duelling scar. As they passed me, one of them gave me a spine-chilling coy look and lifted the hem of her dress up to the knee and I can safely say that the last time I saw a leg that big was when a Punjab butcher showed me half a bullock in a chest freezer. The ghastly ceremony ground to a halt and off we trooped to the reception, which was held in a neo-gothic Co-op hall the size of a Zeppelin paint spray shed that had all the intimacy of Lenin's tomb on a half-day closing. Cheap sherry was served in cracked tumblers – Lord knows who trod the grapes for the tepid brew but in my glass I found a Spanish corn plaster. The boiled ham was so thin you could see the letters BR on the plates. One ancient wit shouted to the waitress, 'You slice the ham and I'll shuffle' – the mother-in-law just sneered and poured junket down his ear trumpet.

What I am about to unfold, dear listener, will chill your blood and knot your tripes with sinews of fear. Where to begin this narrative of horror? It started at Blackpool. I had been strolling along the promenade thinking about this and that – mostly that – when suddenly, from out in the brittle sunshine, I found myself plunged into a dimly-lit cavern wherein I saw rows upon rows of worshippers crouched in maddened expectancy. Their eyes were glazed and their lips were wet and blubbery and the breath from their open orifices hung moistly in the fetid atmosphere. Begrimed awnings parted and a tall man in black clothing stood menacingly in front of a table. His eyes gltted narrowly as he surveyed his throbbing coven. His voice when he spoke was a hoarse whisper and my senses reeled as I heard the words that he spat forth... 'Eyes down for a full house.'

I HEAR O'TOOLE PUT HIS PICK THROUGH A 6000 VOLT CABLE — HOW IS HE? — OH BETTER NOW I WENT TO SEE HIM IN HOSPITAL AND YOU COULD TELL HE WAS RIGHT GLAD TO SEE ME WHY? — HIS EYES LIT UP.

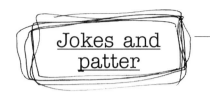

I've died more times than James Cagney ever did.

✩✩✩✩

The only success the mother-in-law ever had
was with the council,
selling her mince pie lids as manhole covers.

✩✩✩✩

If I ever do get worried, I do like they say in the song. 'Grab your coat and get your hat and leave your worries on the doorstep.' Our house is the only one in the street with a doorstep twelve feet high.

✩✩✩✩

Good evening, first of all let me thank you for the wonderful reception you gave me this evening. Not only for the one just now, but for the one you gave me earlier outside when I was busking the queue.

✩✩✩✩

I was in showbusiness for years. Fortunately,
now I'm making a living.

✩✩✩✩

For when I was a young boy and drove my mother wild,
I met a maiden in the woods and she said to me:
'Child – I'm going to show you new game of it's fun
you'll soon evince.' I don't know what it was we played,
but cricket's had it since.

Les as nurse Ada, raising money for children in need.

Because to add to my burden of woe, the mother-in-law came to live with us three months ago. I remember the day well. I hadn't slept the night before. I kept getting the hideous reoccurring nightmare that I was a piece of loose machinery and the wife was chasing me with a spanner and shouting, 'Come here while I tighten your nuts.' I woke up perspiring with horror. The wife was still asleep like a baby with her big toe in her mouth. I bent across her recumbent bulk to kiss her lips. She yawned and with her having no teeth in I felt as if I was peering down the open end of a damp euphomium. What a face. She used to be a model for poison bottles.

○ ○ ○ ○

I had a hell of row with the wife last night. She went on and on about having nothing decent to wear. I said, 'What's wrong with the dress you've got on?' She said, 'Nothing, but with going to work in it, the train and veil's filthy.'

She's got no idea. Last summer she threw away a perfectly good swimming costume, just because it had a hole in the knee. She's got one of her mother's outfits in the wardrobe, but she won't wear it. I wouldn't care, but it only needs the sleeve pressing and the swastikas taking off. Anyway, the argument got worse and when my missus shows her teeth, it makes Jaws look like whitebait. At the finish, she packed her bags and went back to her mother, which didn't do me any good because her mother lives with us. It's not easy for me with those two. They never stop yapping. They say daughters grow to look like their mothers and my wife is no exception. The only difference is the wife's bandy and her mother's knock-kneed. When they stand together in the nude they spell ox. When the wife's mother first came to live with us, the wife shouted upstairs, 'How would you like to speak to my mother?' I said, 'Through a spiritualist, preferably.'

○ ○ ○ ○

Even though my wife is overflowing with good qualities she still has one fault, she's the worlds worst housekeeper. She is the only woman I know that makes the beds with a garden rake, when she fries liver navvies come from far and wide to nail it on their boots. I found her one day in the kitchen bent double and red faced try to screw the top of a steralised bottle of milk. Her idea of spring cleaning is wiping the television screen with a damp cloth, she also insists that hessian curtains are tne best as they will come in handy if another war breaks out. When she washed some spin dry clothes she put tnem on kids still wet and told them run in circles around the garden. When I asked for some poached eggs she stole them from the house next door.

My wife and I were not suited. Her family were so violent they took it in turns to be mugged, while I, the son of a dreamy vicar who was unfrocked because he was found without his clerical collar in a Crewe sauna bath with a masked alderman, I came from a family who could trace their lineage to Elric the Peculiar. Also, physically, my wife is a somewhat large lady. She once collapsed in the middle of the road and until the crane arrived to lift her, the police advised motorists to treat her as a roundabout.

Piano act

We all remember the off-key notes and the started-but-never-finished classical and popular pieces for which Les was famous – not as easy as he made it look!

My parents were determined that I should carry on the family tradition of music. For seven years I sweated away on the piano stool. Then things improved – my dad bought me a piano.

Proposed piano act

[WALK TOWARDS PIANO. SEAT TOO FAR AWAY. PULL PIANO TOWARDS SEAT. BOW TO AUDIENCE. TRY TO OPEN LID, IT'S LOCKED. HAND COMES OUT OF PIANO WITH CROWBAR THEN WRENCHES LID OPEN]

Tonight I would like to devote some time to remembering a forgotten English composer – Seth Bottlecrud. How quickly we forget. Born in a Birmingham laundrette at the age of 40, he was abandoned by his mother who ran off with a lame evangelist. Seth was brought up by Harriet Alsop, an ex-missionary and infamous drunk.

He got a job as water diviner in the Lake District and fell in love with a militant thatcher's aunt who left him for a horse trader in Kendal. He was only three foot tall but joined the Coldstream Guards – he lied about his height. He was in France when the first shot was fired and in Crewe when the second one went off. He wrote some of his best music after being knocked down by a moped on the Great North Road – songs such as 'The Hare and the Pruners' or 'Run Rabbit Run'. Years of living on brewers' yeast and braised turnip ruined his health and in 1938, at the age of ninety, his ears began to ring and when he answered them it was a reverse charge. It was the last straw and quietly without any fuss he went insane and shot a supermarket detective.

He fled to the Pennines and hid in an off-licence where he died after falling into a barrel of whiskey – nobody knows how much he drank but when he was cremated it took ten days to put the fire out. His grave is still on the moors, you can't mistake it. It's the only one with red-nosed tulips – this is the song he wrote as he lay dying...

OPENER — PIANO SPOT   "SEZ LES"

IN MY CONSIDERED OPINION THE TONE OF ENTERTAINMENT
HAS OFTEN BEEN LOWERED BY COMEDIANS TO TRY TO
GET A CHEAP LAUGH BY WEARING A RED NOSE AND
BLOWING RASPBERRIES AT THE AUDIENCE THESE SO
CALLED HUMOURISTS ARE OF COURSE DESTINED FOR
THEATRICAL OBLIVION AND FAILURE.... TONIGHT TO ELEVATE
THE PROGRAMME TO A CULTURAL LEVEL AND TO
FURTHER MY IMAGE AS AN INTELLECTUAL ARTISTE...
I WILL COMMENCE BY RE EVOKING AN EXERCISE IN
MANDIBLE DEXTERITY UPON THE PIANOFORTE — THE PIECE
I AM TO PLAY IS "IN AN 18TH CENTURY DRAWING
ROOM" — PLAY — RED NOSE — RASP.

CARRY
ON

Show two

Main spot with piano

A pious young maiden called Pond
of wearing black garters was fond.
As she said one day, as she knelt down to pray
they're worn in memory of those gone beyond.

I've not always been a brilliant musician. I used to be a tap dancer, but I had to give it up. I kept falling off the sink.

Before I came down here to do the show I was in trouble with the wife. I'd been out and she was waiting up for me, quivering with rage, with her hair in curlers and a mud pack on her face, she looked like a bilious ET. She snarled, 'What do you mean by coming home half drunk?' I said, 'I thought that would have been obvious. I ran out of money.' I asked if my tea was hot, she said, 'It should be, it's been at the back of the fire for an hour.' I call the wife the Lone Ranger because she's always in my pockets looking for silver. One night in bed she shook me and whispered, 'Wake up, you fat fool, there's a burglar going through your trouser pockets.' I said, 'I'm going back to sleep, you can fight it out between you.'

And now, for the benefit of those among you who still haven't had enough of a harrowing experience, I shall make my way to the piano and attempt to destroy whatever sympathy you may have felt for me. The first part of my concert will consist of seventeen works by Chopin. As you may know, Chopin had a relationship with George Sands, which must have been very confusing for Mrs Sands. Of all of Chopin's works, this is my favourite. This polonaise was composed while Chopin was living in Italy so I suppose you could say this was the original spaghetti polonaise.

Les 'serenading' Roy Orbison – if only he had his piano.

Piano act

(PLAY)

— A FUNNY THING HAPPENED TO ME ON THE
WAY TO THE THEATRE. — SO MUCH FOR
MUSIC LESSONS BY POST. YOU'LL NEVER BELIEVE IT, BUT I STARTED
PLAYING THE PIANO WHEN I WAS THREE.
THEN AT THE AGE OF SEVEN — MOTHER LOOKED
AT THE CORNS ON MY HANDS AND DECIDED
TO OPEN THE LID.

BERNARD DELFONT presents :

STAR SHOW '68

PRODUCED BY : MAURICE FOURNIER

Choreography : Denise Shaune

1.	"COME FLY WITH ME"	THE DON PHILLIPS SEXTET
2.	"UP UP AND AWAY"	JOAN SAVAGE
		The Denise Shaune Dancers with Lindy Sarjeant and Mary Devlin introduce
3.	"HAPPY LANDING"	RAY MARTINE
4.	"MUSIC MAN"	THE JIMMY CRAWFORD FOUR
5.	"THE TOPICAL COMEDIAN"	JIM COUTON and REX
6.	"A LOT OF LIVING"	The Denise Shaune Dancers introduce
7.	"FUN TIME"	RAY MARTINE
8.	"HIT PARADE"	DON PARTRIDGE featuring "The Wildfowl"
		INTERVAL
9.	"LIMEHOUSE"	The Denise Shaune Dancers introduce
10.		STEVE MONTGOMERY
11.	"SO RARE"	The Denise Shaune Dancers introduce
12.		JOAN SAVAGE
13.	"TELEVISION'S NEWEST COMEDY STAR"	LES DAWSON
14.	SINGING STAR	SOLOMON KING
15.	FINALE	Full Company

92

SING AT PIANO

There are some things that a man never forgets. His first job for instance... When I left school for six months I became a member of a well-known group, you may have heard of them. They were called the unemployed. I finally got a job on a farm, it was my job to clean out the cow shed. I did my best but I kept putting my foot in it.

I fell in love with the farmer's daughter, Daisy, we called her Daisy because she grew wild in the woods. What a girl, she had braces on her teeth. Every time she kissed me she stapled my lips. She was a big lass, so fat in winter they used her drawers to keep rust off the tractors. She couldn't get in the bath, her mother used to hose her down in the yard.

I tried to impress her with my knowledge of animals. One day I was in the cow shed with a milking stool and a bucket, pulling away like mad and the cow was rolling its eyes and nibbling my ear. Daisy stood at the door with a donkey under her arm – it wasn't a pet, she just had it for kicks. I said, 'I'm doing this well, just look at the contentment on this animal's face, it's really enjoying it.'

She said. 'I'm not surprised, you're milkin' the bull.' I left the farm shortly after that, well the hours were too long and bull wanted to get engaged. I remember my first car. It was so old it was insured for fire, theft and wolf bites. The tyres on it were so shredded everytime I knocked a pedestrian down, he got twenty lashes as he fell. It had a radio in it, I never used it much, it was difficult to drive with earphones on and an accumulator on your knee. What a car. When I went on a main road with it, the cat's eyes used to squint.

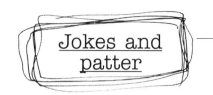

I said to my wife, 'Treasure' – I always call her Treasure,
she reminds me of something that's just been dug up.

She was the flabbiest stripper I've ever seen. When she ran off
the stage she started her own applause.

Just like her mother. Ah, I can see her now, with that funny hat
on, huddled over a steaming cauldron. And then flying out the
window on her broomstick.

The wife in a bikini looks like a pair of pliars in cellotape.

People say to me, 'Cheer up, Lady Luck will smile on you one day.'
By the time she smiles on me she won't have any teeth left.

I wouldn't say she was fat but when she went for a dress fitting,
the assistants worked in shifts.

"I WOULDN'T SAY SHE WAS UGLY" — BUT!

1. HER FACE WAS LIFTED SO OFTEN THEY HAD TO LOWER HER BODY

   •

2. THE MILKMAN FLIRTS WITH ME

   •

3. UNDRESSED WITHOUT DRAWING ROOM CURTAINS AND A PEEPING TOM GAVE HIMSELF UP

   •

4. SO UGLY WENT FOR A SWIM IN LOCH NESS AND THE MONSTER GOT OUT AND PICKETED THE LAKE

   •

5. TRIED TO KISS THE BLARNEY STONE AND IT SPIT AT HER

   •

6. THE MISSING LINK WAS HER PEN PAL

   •

7. WENT TO A HORROR FILM — AUDIENCE THOUGHT SHE WAS MAKING A PERSONAL APPEARANCE

   •

Blankety Blank

Remember all the hilarious introductions, the asides, the fillers… With some of these sketches we have included Les's notes and jibes.

Blankety Blank

Yes, fellow Britons, it's *Blankety Blank* again, the show that puts more people sleep than Ovaltine. Have we got prizes tonight… Have we? This evening, lucky competitors can win a week's holiday down a Ugandan tin mine. We have a do-it-yourself brain surgery kit with matching curtains, a faulty water bed for a married couple who are drifting apart and last but not least…

Welocme to Blankety Blank....the show that has **prooved** beyond any shadow of doubt that there is life after drivel.
Please keep sending your comments on the prgramme ~~mxixxbxaxxxtxpcoxxxpxingxthxx~~ ~~txxbxxxxxxxxdxxxdxxixxx~~ we like to receive them and the bricks tgere tied to come in handy.
Getting interesting **pepple** to come on the show as panellists is very difficult... ~~xxxxxxdxxfxtxxrxghxtxrixxxxxx~~ as you can imagine....if tonight is anything to go by it's ~~txpxxxxxxx~~becoming impossible.
We have wonderful prizes to be won...as you know the B.B.C spare no expense when they advetise for scra p....~~xxxdxxbxxxxyxx~~ so lets get on with it....

Blankety Blank

Here's one for our younger viewers. Mary had a little bear, it loved her because she was kind. Everywhere that Mary went. she had a bear behind. Well, having proved once again that if laughter is infectious then I've found a cure, let's meet our guest-star panel for this evening. With celebrities like this there's only one thing to say: 'Mayday! Mayday!'

What a show. I wouldn't give this spot to a dry cleaner.

I've seen his act and believe me, he's got a wonderful future behind him.

He's never allowed obscurity to stop him being a failure.

I'm not going to say anything disparaging about our celebrity panel. You can see for yourselves that we're having trouble getting people.

What a singer... she's been charged with cruelty to tonsils/ears.

Blankety Blank

Good evening ladies and gentlemen and to those of you who thirst for culture, welcome, welcome indeed to a new series of *Blankety Blank*, the cut-price BBC show that possesses all the radiant charm wit and sophistication usually only associated with the ritual mating dance of the East Malay dung beetle.

Time now to meet our distinguished panel of celebrities. We thought it would be nice to go out and find a really glittering cavalcade of stars for this first show in the new series and I think you'll agree by what we've got that we must have been looking in the wrong direction. The last time I saw faces like theirs was in a tank full of trout.

Blankety Blank

Show seven.

My wife works as a blacksmith's assistant, it's a fairly easy job,
when the shoes are ready the wife hands the blacksmith the horse.
1 was in the forge the other day and 1 thought to myself, where have
all the craftsmen gone...A fellow called to my house last week, he
looked a bit peculiar, his chin jutted out like a platelayer's shovel
and 1've seen such big ears...he looked like a wingnut...He said:
"Do you want any skilled jobs doing?" I said oh are you are you a
handyman? He said oh 1'm handy alright, 1 only live round the corner.
He said 1'm a highly specialized painter...1 said well you can put an
undercoat on the garden shed, creosalt the fence and paint my porch.
He came back threehours later and charged me twenty pounds...He said
oh by the way, you have'nt got a porch, it's a B.M.W.
On with a show that is a craft in it's self...Blankety Blank....

98

Every actor waits for his ship to come home. He's been waiting so long the pier's collapsed.

He firmly believes in the saying, 'If at first you don't succeed – stick 'em up.'

Welcome to *Blankety Blank* and having just seen the prizes we have you are welcome to it.

People often ask where we get the prizes for *Blankety Blank*. Have you ever heard of War on Want?

They laughed at Edison Bell's telephone, they laughed at Stevenson's rocket. He's trying to find out who wrote their script.

Good Evening culture hunters and welcome to a new series of Blankety Blank... From the mist shrouded Hebbides to the storm tossed cliffs of Cornwall, hardy Britons are impatiently sitting on the edge of their seats for a style of entertainment that has given a new meaning to the word "Cheap".

Blankety Blank

For the benefit of our younger viewers, here are some jokes that made your parents laugh. I was in a restaurant the other day. I called the waiter over and said, 'Waiter, there's a fly in my soup. What's it doing there?' He said, 'The breast stroke.' I said, 'Get it out.' He said, 'There's no need to, sir, the spider on your bread will get it.'

Well, there's one thing about those jokes, it proves that the good old days weren't. Welcome to another new series of *Blankety Blank*. Do you like the new-look set? It's a replica of Caligua's council flat.

Sometimes we get a panel of celebrities who give you a run for your money, others are more subtle and plant the seeds of comedy. Tonight's panel falls between the two, they've all run to seed. May I introduce...

A young man who knows no fear, a young man who once drove a motorcycle over three buses and walked away after his feat with pride and a broken collarbone. He's a sort of swashbuckler – the trouble is now his swash is beginning to buckle. Eddie Kidd.

Anneka Rice – with a name like that I wish she'd put her head on my pilau. I'd know what to do because my poppadum told me and I'm not about to curry favour.

An elegant lady who's come on by leaps and bounds – her agent's a kangaroo. She's a fine comedienne and actress. I forget what else she told me to say. Janet Brown.

Show 13

Good Evening and welcome again to Blankety Blank, and for the bemaift
of students of history, here are some of the jokes from my act.
A fellow said to me the other day, how's the wife, 1 said compared to what?
What a woman 1 got home last night and she had a come to bed look about her...
she'd took her teeth out.

She has'nt got an ounce of passion innher...the only time she gets a glint in
her eye is when whe) gets a shock off the electric blanket.
Yxxxxxxxxxxxxx On our honeymoon xxxxxxxxxxxxxxxx in cornwall she fell down
a wishing well, 1 was amazed 1 did'nt know they worked.
Well it's quite obvious that they did'nt work, but we do have a panel that does
xxxxxxxxxxxxxxxxxxxxxxx six celebritires who are electrifying, and you'll
have a shock when you see them.....Which proves that this show has become
television's knacker'smyard.

Blankety Blank

It's Blankety Blank once more and all over the nation, viewers are sat in front of their sets in case anybody tries to switch them on. Here's a joke to get us fallin about....A man in a job centre heard a voice say: Give us a job... lokked down a duck with a trilby on...he did'nt take much notice at first, if it had been a goose, he's have had another gander....Job no good to me I'M a bricklayer....all the studio audince is falling about but the exit's shut. Please hello to a great team of celebrities....when you look at them it's like an old fairy story....Grim. We're not scraping the barrel anymore, we're gving it an undercoat.

Good evening and welcome to a new series of *Blankety Blank*, the effervescent bubbling cauldron of uninhibited merriment that possesses all the charm and intellectualism usually associated with a geriatric parrot.I would like to take this opportunity to thank the BBC for letting me work on the show once more and secondly to thank a rather ugly tax demand for making it necessary...

While I'm at it, I'd like to say something to all the nurses at Preston Royal hospital who during my recent incarceration there poked pillaged and plundered my helpless body with blanket baths. I'd just like to say, 'Girls... Ooh, ooh, why don't you do house calls?'

Blankety Blank

Every celebrity on the panel tonight is a headliner: they worry about being out of work so often they've got lines on their heads.

A fine performer who's been in showbusiness for years. The girls chase him even now, but he always gives them their purses back. Give him the moonlight, give him the girl and leave the rest to his leg. Frankie Vaughan.

Please meet a lovely lass who started at the bottom but is slowly working herself up to obscurity. I've offered to help her career but she won't take my hotel room key. Fern Britton.

Another beautiful maiden. The last time she appeared on *Blankety Blank* she was absolutely fanastic. Then I let her out of my dressing room. She was offered a leading role in *Dallas* but wouldn't change her name to Howard Keel. Lesley Judd.

Blankety Blank

Nice to have an old mate on the show, he's a comedian who can remember everytime he got a laugh – 1965, 1978 and 1983. I saw him doing cabaret in a restaurant once and the audience was doubled up. It's a terrible thing, salmonella. Charlie Williams.

Another dear friend whose first appearance on a stage was interrupted by the Prime Minister. Our guest didn't mind. She liked Disraeli. I'm not saying she's been around a long time, but the last time she entertained the troops she caught a chill at Bannockburn. Aimi MacDonald.

An old mate and a fellow Water Rat. He's appeared in the pantomime *Mother Goose* so often every time he walks on the stage they give him the bird. Paul Shane.

A lovely lady with an arresting personality, but when I got hold of her for a gentle touch she handcuffed me. Jill Gascoine.

Since his last appearance on this show we've received two thousand letters asking for him to came back and anyone who can pay that sort of money out for stamps deserves to come back. Tony Blackburn.

They say that Faith can move mountains and the way she's built they'd have to make room for her. Faith Brown.

I keep hoping we'll get together after the show, after all, anything she can do I dando better. Susan Dando.

One of Les's many Blankety Blank *shows, starring Jane Marie Osbourne, Peter Goodwright, Jean Boht, John Craven, Aimi Macdonald and Stan Boardman.*

Monologue

Did you know that there are more accidents in the home than there are on the roads? In most cases the household injuries are caused by neglect or carelessness, but quite a few are the result of people keeping pets and one animal in particular is a menace – the common or garden hamster. And that is why I am the vice chairman of a society that is trying to get the Government to pass a law making it compulsory for hamsters to be kept on a lead, or in the case of an invalid hamster, a seat belt.

Allow me to give you a graphic illustration of how dangerous hamsters can be. Every evening before she gets into bed, my wife's mother likes to stand in front of an open window and play a snatch of 'Carnival in Venice' on a bugle. She varies her programme from time to time with either a selection from Gilbert and Sullivan or punk rock. The other night a hamster belonging to one of my neighbours ran upstairs to her bedroom and, as the last strains of 'HMS Pinafore' were dying away, the rodent shot up the mother-in-law's nightdress and bit her on a semibreve. Not unnaturally, she leapt in the air like a frog on a hot plate and fell out of the window. Fortunately for her, her corsets snagged on the latch of the transom and she began to swing backwards and forwards still playing the bugle.

To say the least, it was a tricky situation, I tired to haul her in, but she was far too heavy for me to shift even with a block and tackle from Wimpey. A passing vagrant from Uganda at my request climbed a stunted laburnum, held her legs and jumped down to the ground with her. Alas, her corsets, being of the pre-war type with elasticated panels, stretched like a catapult and propelled her up to the guttering and on the way she broke a fan light and ruptured a thrush. The vagrant sustained a fractured elbow, lost his teeth down a drain and ran off shouting 'General Amin's a puff.'

With the help of a traffic warden and a drunk, we managed to stop her bouncing up and down and a boy scout stood on my shoulders and tried to saw through her corsets with his bowie knife. Unfortunately, she was till playing the bugle and deafened him with the song 'Goodbye Dolly Gray'. The lad panicked and cut through his woggle. The traffic warden got fed up and put a ticket on a milk float. The drunk was sick in a bed of gladioli and I gave it up and went in to have a laugh at *Crossroads*. All night she went up and down, I couldn't sleep with the noise of her head banging on the gable end. The following day a tom cat clawed up under her nightdress and yowled in sheer terror. I don't know what he saw, but he was last seen trying to break into a vasectomy clinic. Finally, she struggled out of her bondage and fell off.

LES DAWSON

Where was 1 oh yes the letter from a grateful member of the public...
It reads very simply:

          Dear Sir,
               You have done more for me than any specialist
          for years 1 have suffered from acute insomnia, my
          nights abed were a restless misery, 1 have had
          treatment in clinics at Zurich ̶b̶a̶s̶e̶ basle and
          Rhly but to no ̶a̶v̶a̶i̶l̶ avail. ̶A̶l̶l̶x̶x̶a̶n̶d̶x̶t̶h̶e̶n̶x̶1̶x
          saw you on the GOOD OLD DAYS and 1 could'nt keep
          my eyes open...

          but you Mr Dawson cured
                              me

LES DAWSON

was in partnersnip with merlin.

Went to see our doctor, l·m not saying he's old fashioned but when he lances a boil, he does it on horseback...Actually he'll have to retire shortly he's running out of leaches...xxxxxxxxxxxxxxxxxxxxxxxxxxxxxx he's not a weathly doctor even his stetescpe's on a party line... Anyway l went into his surgeryhe was sat down trying to turn base metal into gold...l shouted Good Morning, because he's so deaf he's got sterio in his ear trumpet...He said xxxxxxxxxxxxxxxxxxxxxxxxxxxxxxxxxxxxx what seems to be the trouble? l said l get a lot of chest colds these days and a sore throat...he said do you smoke l said yes he said thats the trouble, next time you want a ciagrette have a piece of chocolate instead l said l·ve tried that but l could slight the chocolate...l said but the main reason l·ve come is recently l stayed in some dirty digs and xxxxxxx ever since l've been bitten by a virulent type of body lice he said well don·t worry go home and put sugar on them, l said will that kill ·em he said no its rots their teeth.....

GRAND THEATRE
BLACKPOOL

LAUGH WITH LES
Summer season, 1984

Les worked hard at his introductions and openers. The leader of his orchestra was often the butt of his jokes, as were his guests – they all knew what to expect…

I must say that it's a great pleasure to be here this evening in this superbly-furnished example of an early Victorian knacker's yard, appearing before such a handsome, well-dressed audience and listening to this fine resident orchestra. And that's one thing you'll find about me, I'm always polite – as well as tone deaf with eye trouble.

It's great working again with [NAME OF BANDLEADER]. It's six years since I worked with him last and he's gained a little weight in the interim… and quite a lot in the outer rim too. Singers like working with him because he picks up things fast. Like the cigarette girl we had here last week. You couldn't pick up anything faster than her.

Let's have a big hand for the drummer. He got married on Monday. [APPLAUSE] And now a big hand for his wife – the bass player! The boys in the band don't look too great just now because they were up half of the night playing strip poker… and most of them have shocking colds. But they're a great bunch of boozers. The only band I know whose signature is 'Tea for Two… and Black Coffee for the Rest'.

Show 2

Tonight, ladies and gentlemen, I'd like to talk about wildlife and by that I don't mean my marriage. Some time ago I met a naturalist who cured badgers of chilblains by wrapping their feet in poultices made of pith from the skins of citrus fruits. In fact he's the only man I know who can take the pith out of grapefruits.

"SEZ LES"...SHOW TWO...OPENING PATTER.

Out of the second world war, came many stories of valour...from Dunkirk to Normandy, the spirit of Britain was a burning torch of defiance in the teeth of the jackbooted tyranny that threatened to engulf our green and mortgaged land...One story that has never been told outside of the War Office, sums up for all time the stolicism of our island heritage. It concerns the exploit of flying officer Everett Gumboil Hxxwxxx Gumboil stood six foot four never smoked or drank or went out with women and he made all his own frocks. His remarks about the the Battle Of Britain, xxxxxwill be told for ever..."If those awful Germans don't go away, l'll simply dissolve with fury!' In 1944, he was flying one of ten Spitfires who were going over Germany to drop leaflets. All the planes returned with the exception of xxxxxxxx Lavender Gumboil's...all night the station waited, but he never returned. Four week's later gloom had settled among his comrades. his commanding said: "He may have been an old fruit, but he was'nt a bad sort old Lavender...sort of miss his chanel number nine floating around the bogs. Thre months later, an air force sentry, washing his bayonet frog in the ablitions, heard the drone of a Spitfire...he rushed out and lo a miracle...Lavender Gumboil was coming home. The entire station stood to attention as Gumboil daintily stepped from the aircraft. Hi you all look so cuddly in your blues...Gumboil old chap, broadly speaking of course...how are you what was it like...Gumboil said oh the noise the people...His commanding officer said but what happened all the others came straight back after dropping their leaflets...Gumboil sniffed and said dropped the leaflets...oh l went round putting them through the ixt letter boxes...

Proposed Opening.

From the storm tossed Hebrides to the pastoral tranquility of the
Cotswolds; from the wind buffeted shores of East Anglia to the rolling
majesty of the Mendips, Great Britain is a land of complex geographical
contrasts....One's pride in a lake-land tarn is a devout as the passion
expressed towards a Cornish seascape. Some years ago l lost myself in
the xxxxyxxxxxxx rustic balm of Dorset, Hardy's Wessex...Even now l
thirst for yet another glimpse of moonlight dappling the calm waters of
Poole harbour, to see again the craggy indifference of Lulworth Cove.
One night xxxxxxxx l rested beneath the frowning outline of Corfe
Castle, who's ruins were thrown in stark relief against a pallid skyline
As l smoked a reflective briar l mused on the history that this old
bastion had lived through...in my imagination, l heard the clatter of
broadswords and smelt the tang of burnished leather...Just then from
a hole in the wall of the inner keep. came the figure of a tall man
sombrely dressed in a thinning ulster, opera cape and sensible gaiters.
He nodded curtly and began to play on a Stradivarus, a haunting melody
that echoed across the bridge of time...Its lilt clamped my throat
in an agony of extasy, and when the last refrian had melted into the
dusk, l said to him, what a beautiful piece of music...who wrote it
He answered softly, l did...Have you had it published l replied. No
he said nobody will touch it. Nonsense l retorted angrily, allow me
to take a copy to London. l will beseech the tunesmiths of Charing
Cross to publish it so that the world may share my experience. He
gave me a soiled copy from up his cardigan and retraced his steps back
into the shadows of the keep...l called after him Pray inform me sir
what is the name of your music, and his voice floated on the nightair
"Its called, l love you so much my piles smart.

The Val Doonican Show

Good evening ladies and gentlemen. I would like to play for you now that memorable ballad that is ever in our thoughts, and it is of course the unforgettable song... called 'unforgettable'.... [play] Actually I had intended to play a little something from Mozart but I thought, why the hell should I? He never plays any of mine. Then I toyed with the idea of strumming a few bars of Ravel's 'Pavan por Infante Defunct' but to be honest I couldn't remember by the sound of it if it was a tune or a Latin prescription for nappy rash.

.

Les in full flow with John Lander, Mayor of Blackpool, 1986.

INTRO: GUYS AND DOLLS

It cannot have escaped your notice, ladies and gentlemen, that most of the guest on this show are not what you would call how can I put it? Young... Syd Lawrence, for instance, between numbers is wont to sit in his bath chair reeking of Fiery Jacket and longing for a blanket bath.

Humphrey Lyttleton talks about the time he appeared on the Royal Command Performance... before the Queen and Prince Albert. In fact this show makes the *Good Old Days* look like *New Faces*. I'd put my foot down, but the gout's killing me.

My next guests, I am told, are 134 years of age. Mind you, there are six of them... Ladies and gentlemen, clap your hands over your ears for the Guys And Dolls.

OPENING SCRIPT SHOW FOUR.
SEZ LES AUTUMN 1976 SERIES

LES: "Braised fruit in trousers smoulder
Gone, gone like the earache of August
Time liken to a raped Hippo on tin...dropping,
dropping...faces like tins of comdemed veal
lies groping the morrow...come and jock up
the strap"

That beautiful tone poem, written in 1968 introduces our tribute toniight
to the author of it...ⅩⅩⅩⅩⅩⅩⅩⅩⅩⅩⅩⅩⅩⅩⅩ The only son of
an Egyptian bingo addict from Grimsby, he was a poet composer and the
first man ever to cure a duck of chilblains...His name, Mustapha Fettle.
ⅩⅩⅩⅩⅩⅩ He was born ⅩⅩⅩⅩⅩⅩⅩ during a winter that was so cold,
brass monkeys were putting out tenders to welders...His mother who was
a ⅩⅩⅩⅩⅩⅩ gave birth to him in a field of frozen lettuce, they
could'nt lie her down because of the intense cold, so it was a case of
stand and deliver...

Syd Lawrence

Eight years ago, when we first started doing the show *Sez Les*, we looked
around for a cheap resident orchestra. We couldn't find one anywhere until
one night we got a phone call from a tone-deaf plumber who said there was a
band who played in a Derby and Joan club during lectures on the *Kama
Sutra*. We went there and found the Syd Lawrence orchestra. In those far-off
days, the band was described by the critics as a minor disaster. But since
then they've played all over the country and I can safetly say that the band
is now a major disaster. Syd still plays the same trumpet he's had for years.
It's so old it was once used for medieval pregnancy tests. But here he is, with
the aid of Gary Husband on drums with...

Les Dawson Opening

ZOOM DOWN ON STUDIOS — SHOT OF AUDIENCE
BEING WHIPPED INTO THE STATION FOYER — INSIDE whips
for stars on sunday — some for j/show — one for "sez les"
~~some~~ PEOPLE ON KNEES BEGGING TO BE ~~ALLOWED~~ /FREE
(JUNIOR SHOWTIME "
TO SEE "STARS ON SUNDAY" AND CRIES OF
"OH NO — NOT "SEZ LES" AGAIN! — THEN BEING
DRAGGED ~~OFF~~ — ANNOUNCER (JOHN CLEESE) INTO
SHOT: "WELCOME TO THE MAKE-BELIEVE WORLD OF
TELEVISION — (IN BACKGROUND PEOPLE BEING
DRAGGED INSIDE — (SHOT OF THREE GALLOWS
(TV CRITICS) — JOHN COME IN — IN THESE
STUDIOS MANY BIG BUDGET SHOWS TAKE
PLACE — (BIG GLITTERING "S ON SUNDAY SET)
            BIG "JUNIOR SHOWTIME WITH STARS
            BIG GLAMOROUS ~~ENTROBENT~~ AARM

    ___ CUT TO CUPBOARD OR WHAT EER.
        ___ "CRIES OF FOOD — FOOD
            ___ "SEZ LES" SET   PTO

SHOT OF LES ARGUING WITH WRITERS AND
PRODUCER _____ WALK ONTO SET
            BIG ~~SCALES — WALK ON SET~~)
WITH DANCERS — "(~~WALK ONTO A STAIR~~)

                    "STAIRWAY TO PARADISE"
                    ___ . ___

118

LES DAWSON

Ladies and Gentlemen, there is an old adgge that says:Music hath
charm to sooth the savage beast, l'd like to introduce you now to an
orchestra that once drove a hamster raving mad...there are many great
bands, and this one really grates...Directed by Mr Ivor Raymonde of
whom Sir Thomas Beecham once said..Who? This wonderful orchestra who
last worked on a troops concert at Bannockburn, will get the show
moving to its customary deteriation with.........

Well its been a pleasure having you and the boys...boys, more like
a strike picket from a wintergreen factory...No but seriously Ivor,
thanks for coming along and as one musician to another, may l say
that listening to your piano work is like having a birthday,it put
years on me...Just to show you how it xhxuxix shpuld be done....move xixx
over before the M.U. endorse your card...

Show four

Opener

Last week I went on a pilgrimage to a high plateau in Northern
Uganda. I had gone to place a wreath of hyacinths on the humble
mound that marks the final resting place of my uncle. He went to
Africa as a salesman for a Scottish rissole company. He was a fine
man. He stood six-foot six-inches in his string vest. He lived with a
tribe of pygmies and did very well for himself. He opened a blow
pipe service station and on Thursdays he ran a pontoon school in a
loin cloth laundry. One day, against the advice of the pygmies he set
out to sell health foods to cannibals – bravely, he marched into
their village and gave the cannibal chief a nut fritter. He was never
seen again. Nobody knows what happened but all that was found
was his spats, a collar stud, a bottle of grape water and a spoonful
of chutney. The pygmies never forgot his bravery and they erected
a simple stone on his grave with this moving inscription: 'Twit'.

(I)

Good Evening, Buenos noches, guten abend...that means good eveing in three
languages....carbolic acid that means good bye in any language.
Welcome to Blankety Blank always difficult to descirbe this show but if
entertainment was elastic there would'nt be enough in this show for a frog's
jockstrap. However let us meet our distinguished panel of celebrities
                    (InTro) 1 call them celebrities but it's only in fun

~~Xxxxxxxxxxxxxxxxxxixxthatx~~

    Aiden J Harvey: When 1 first saw this young man's act, 1 was on the the floor
                    it was the only place to stretch out for a kip.

    Clare Raynor: A fine lady who's sound advice has been followed by people like
                    Crippen Mussolini the captain of the Titanic....she still has'nt
                    given me a winner.

    Tracey Dorning: A super actress from a super family films, stage plays
                    television shows...she auditions for them all..

    Bernie Winters: a comedian who can have you laughing one minute then crying
                    for the next hour when variety died they held his act for
                    questioning....

    Sally James: A young lady who had the chance to star in the film:Long
                    Hohn Silver but did'nt think it was worth having aleg off for

    Nicholas Parsons: Our next celebrity started out in show business as a bouncer
                    in a Liverpool branch of Mothercare...one of nicest men 1've
                    ever met and when he had his own quiz show *IN THE FIRST YEAR OF IT MORE T/V SETS*
Well having met our star oanel 1 think you'll agree that there s only one thing
1 can say to our contestants and that is....May Day May Day....

*WERE SOLD
THAN
ANY
OTHER
— I SOLD MINE
FOR A
STARS*

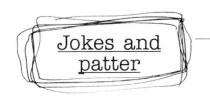

Jokes and patter

I went to the tailor the other week. I said,
'Where's the cheapest cloth in the shop?'
He said, 'You're wearing it.'
I said to him, 'What can I have for £50?'
He gave me some wool and a loom.
He said, 'For £150 I can do you a nice suit but
the extras will be £20.
I said, 'Why will I need extras?'
He said, 'You'll want sleeves, won't you?'

☆☆☆☆

I went to a small guest house. The manager said,
'You want a room with running water?
I said, 'What do you think I am?
A trout?'

☆☆☆☆

So there you are. If you want security, buy a house.
People will always give you the same advice,
there's money in property,
which sounds logical. But have you ever tried to pay
the rates with a brick?

☆☆☆☆

I wouldn't say the room was small but you had to buy bananas
ready peeled.

There was an old farmer from Greece
Who did terrible things to his geese
But he went too far with a budgerigar
And the parrot phoned the police.

LES DAWSON

Manchester born Les Dawson started out as an electrician, then in succession became an insurance agent, vacuum salesman, warehouseman and pub pianist.

After army service as a gunnery-driver in a tank regiment, he took a course on English composition and lived in London and Paris trying to sell short stories.

Les also found time to perform in clubs and pubs as a singer, and to develop his highly original comedy line. An audition led to radio work and to three northern T.V. shows. Top flight night clubs took an interest in Les who also wrote two short comedies for the B.B.C.

Married, with two children, Les lives in Unsworth near Bury, after having travelled most of the continent with his family.

When I was a schoolboy at Eton, I fagged for a sixth former called Harcourt Wimberry. He was of course the son of Archibald Wimberry, the well-known haemorrhoid ointment millionaire. A man who started at the bottom and did very well out of it. Dare one say that he had indeed made a pile?

Harcourt Wimberry was the most cowardly boy I ever met; he was so frightened of personal injury that he used to wear a seat belt when he went to the toilet. For his age he was quite small, in fact, when he pulled his socks up, he blindfolded himself.

After I had left school to take up my appointment as a junior vet with a Jesuit mission steel band in Borneo, it was my task to prevent the natives from injecting a paralysing fluid in goats' bottoms in order to mate them with Indonesian owls. It was a disgusting practice and all they ever got was a dead-end kid that didn't give a hoot. One night as I sat sipping a mint julep with my friend the very reverend Clyde Potts on the verandah of a permissive laundrette in Rangoon, the conversation turned to the effects of snake bites on a cow's udder, not much of a chat really, it was neither one fang nor the udder.

Potts suddenly, while beating a dung beetle to death with a coat hanger, said, 'Harcourt Wimberry is now famous as a big game hunter.' I was staggered by the news, he of all people braving the ferocity of wild life?

Two months later I went home and a grateful government gave me a photograph of Wedgewood Benn and a place in a dole queue. One night I went to a party and there in a corner stood Harcourt Wimberry, older greyer and smaller, he made a fuss over me and I couldn't resist telling him of my surprise at hearing that he was a big game hunter.

He said, 'Would you like to see my trophies?'

I said, 'Yes,' and the following day he took me to his house.

In his study he pointed to a wall and said, 'There is the fruit of my big game hunting. I finally overcame my cowardice by facing those wild beasts.'

I looked on the wall and all I could see was a tusk, a clump of hair and a broken rhino horn. I said, 'When you go hunting what do you use?'

He said, 'Hand grenades.'

○ ○ ○ ○

Daddy was never in showbusiness. He was an old soldier. For years he was in the cavalry. Mind you, the only charge he was on was for vagrancy. I've never known a man who hated work as much as he did. I know for a fact he suffered from nightmares. He kept having terrible dreams about full employment. And I'm told that in the hunger march from Jarrow in the 1930s, he was the only one singing. He spent so much time in bed that when he had to get up to visit the bathroom he got travel sickness.

I don't honestly think he liked me very much because when I was seven I had wax in my ears and, let's face it, any other father would have taken his son to a clinic. Not mine: he stood me in a saucer and use me as a night light. I asked him once why it was that his neck was dirtier than mine. He said, 'It's bound to be, you little twit. I'm older than you.'

○ ○ ○ ○

[SING: 'PEOPLE']

Yes, ladies and gentlemen, people, that is what living is all about, meeting people, knowing people and, as we go through life, it's people who colour our world, who form the basis of our understanding. Friend and foe alike, they forge the blade of our increasing knowledge. The first people I recall were my parents. I remember my father looking at me with tears in his eyes and saying sadly, 'You'll have to go son, I can no longer support you.' With that he put me in my pram and pushed it down the M1. Mother was furious, she said, 'You can't let let him go like that, he's only two. Run after him and give him a list of digs.'

Some people one can never forget. Years ago when I discovered that the wife was a deserter from the Black Watch the shock of it sent me for treatment to a psychiatrist. I lay on his coach and told him about my reoccurring nightmare in which I dreamed that the mother-in-law was chasing me with a crocodile. I could feel the hot rancid breath on my neck, the snapping of those great decayed teeth, the yellow eyes full of primeval malice. The psychiatrist went pale. He said, 'That's terrible.' I said, 'That's nothing, wait until I tell you about the crocodile.'

Thank you and may I say how glad I am to receive such a tumultuous welcome. I must say, after some of the receptions I've had lately, if they haven't started throwing things by now, I'm a roaring success.

You know, it isn't easy for me to think of funny things to say, as you'll no doubt notice if you stay awake long enough, and it's only by sheer hard work and perseverance that I've become what I am today. A dismal failure. I haven't always been a dismal failure though. I was once a cheerful failure. When I first started as an unemployed actor, I used to worry if nobody laughed when I said something funny. Now I worry when they do – I wonder where they've heard it before.

I used to think a lot of my mother and every night I'd go out and get a bunch of flowers. It took a lot of courage to break into the cemetary after dark.

Ah, my mother. I can see her now. A little grey-haired old lady with a picture of my father close to her heart. She was proud of that tattoo. My mother. It's true, you know, there is something about a mother. There was something about mine. I think it was the smell. And worry. She used to worry about everything. She worried about my granddad being lonely. He was lonely too. He'd been dead fifteen years. Mind you, he hung on until the very end. One-hundred-and-thirty, he was. He refused to die until he'd found an undertaker who gave green stamps.

All that worry goes back to that eventful day one spring when the British Medical Association, the RSPCA and Her Majesty's Customs and Excise attended my christening. My mother loved telling me about it. She'd pick me up, put me on her knee, take a drag of her clay pipe and tell me all about it. How she dressed me up in a little shawl and proudly wheeled me up to the church in a rusty wheelbarrow. It had to be the wheelbarrow. My brother had gone for some coal in the pram.

Les as W.C. Fields, his hero.

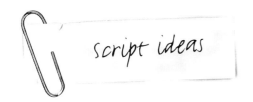
script ideas

Sometimes Les would scribble ideas into his notebooks but here is a selection of gags that he's organised under general topics.

Script idea one

Showbusiness

My great aunt Margaret, just before she died at the ripe old age of ninety-eight, called me to her bedside and whispered, nephew, if you ever fail to get a laugh as a comedian I shall turn over in my grave. That was ten years ago. Yesterday I attended a seance in Birmingham. The medium went into a deep trance and said, 'I don't know for whom this concerns but I'm getting a very strange message through from someone called Spinning Maggie.' Maggie was a wonderful person, actually. She was the last of the gaiety girls in Edwardian London. Men used to drink champagne from her slipper and throw roses at her as she danced. She was fifty-nine when she retired... with damp feet and greenfly.

Although I come from a showbusiness family, I wasn't born in a suitcase at the back of a theatre. I was born in hospital. It was when my father saw me that he put me in a suitcase. For years my father toured the music halls doing an act that was a mixture of Sophie Tucker and Fred Astaire. He didn't do very well because the trouble was he sang like Fred Astaire and danced like Sophie Tucker. In fact he was on the public assistance so often, they asked him to MC their staff dances.

Script two

Politics

It's not widely know that showbusiness isn't the only thing I've been unemployed at. Indeed, I have always taken a keen interest in politics. I once stood as a Liberal candidate in a local by-election. You know what a Liberal is, don't you? That's a Conservative who lives in a council house. I didn't do very well – I only got three votes and that was after a recount. I blame the wife for it. She went canvassing householders for me. I found out later she said to them, 'Give my husband a vote – he's no idea, but we can't afford to lose the deposit.'

I campaigned on the subject of slum property. The only trouble was the only slum in the district was mine... But I did all the things that candidates do. I went round kissing babies and patting dogs on the head – I was off work three months with hard pad and nappy rash. I picked one little fellow up, gave him a cuddle and he turned round and belted me. It turned out he was a jockey going to Newmarket.

"PROPOSED SCRIPT."   25

THANK YOU LADIES & GENTLEMEN

POOR?

HOUSE

SOME FOLK CRINGE

I DON'T FEEL SO

ITS OFTEN SAID THAT AN ARTIST CAN TELL HOW WELL KNOWN HE IS BY THE AMOUNT OF APPLAUSE HE RECIEVES — IF THATS TRUE ALL THATS LEFT FOR ME TO SAY IS — THANK YOU, STRANGERS.

PLEASE DON'T TAKE OFFENCE — it's only joking — THATS THE TROUBLE WITH MY ACT

129

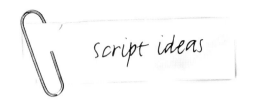
script ideas

Script three

Crime and the criminal

There's no doubt about it that crime is on the increase. An old maid where I live was held up the other night by a robber. He snarled, 'Give me all your money.' She said, 'I haven't got any.' And with that he started to run away. She called after him, 'Come back this minute! And if you search me again I'll write a cheque out for you.'

Mind you, I live in a very tough district. The other morning I saw an old man of eighty lying on the floor and six big fellows with clubs were hitting him. A woman said to me, 'Why don't you go and break it up?' I said, 'Why should I? After all, you don't know who started it.'

It really is a terrible area. The only holiday the kids get at the local school is on Al Capone's birthday. The little lad across the road last week shot his parents so that he could go on an orphan's picnic. And there's so many fiddles going on at the local bingo hall, Mantovani calls out the numbers. One of my neighbours has spent years in jail. In fact, he was only released a month ago and they missed him so much at the prison they asked him to go back part time.

Script four

Sport and sportsmen

[AT PIANO: PLAY 'SKATER'S WALTZ']

...Thin ice. I'm fond of all physical activities. I used to think nothing of running six miles before breakfast ten years ago. And I don't think so much of it now. But sport is a part of the British heritage. As Captain Webb said as he sank for the third time in the channel – 'Glub, glub...'

I come from a family of sportsmen. My grandfather was a boxer and grandmother was a cocker spaniel . In his earlier fighting days, granddad was known as 'washing day' because he was always hanging over the ropes. He was on the canvas so often he changed his name to Battling Rembrandt. He was the only boxer ever who had a cauliflower rear. In his last fight, he created a sensation – no gum shield, no gloves, no shorts. My uncle Joe was an Olympic shot-putter, but in Mexico he got disqualified. No wonder – you should have seen where he was putting it.

Les at work in his study, with the typewriter on which he wrote so many of his sketches.

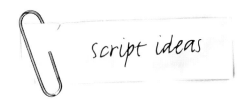
script ideas

Script five

Marriage

When I was courting the wife, intimate friends of mine begged me not to marry her. They said, 'You're not suited and if you feel that you are falling in love with her – fight it, fight it.' If I'd known then what I now now, I'd have shot it. I met her in a discount store in London. I went in for a lampshade and I said to her, 'What will you take off for cash?' She said, 'Everything bar my earrings.' I'll never forget the night I proposed to her. We were sat in her back garden. Her mother had just finished the washing and we sat holding hands and watching the moon go down over her father's underpants.

I got down on one knee and whispered, 'Beloved, will you marry me?' She hesitated as she puffed at her pipe. I cried, 'You hesitated, my angel! Don't tell me there's someone else.' She looked at me and said, 'Oh my God. There's *got* to be...' I went in to see her mother. 'Madam,' I said, 'I want to marry your daughter.' She said, 'Certainly, son, but can you keep her?' I said, 'Why, is she going bad?'

Script six

In-laws

The biggest tragedy about getting married is that you can't choose your in-laws. I had a look at my wedding photographs the other night and, I'm not joking, the wife's family look like a mafia convention. I'm stood at the side of her mother and with her being big and wearing a white coat it looks as if I'm squatting at the foot of an alp. What a woman – I took her to a zoo one week and every time she walked past the lion's cage, the lion picked up a chair and whip.

Every time she comes to visit us the flowers on the sideboard wilt – and they're plastic. She never stops talking: last winter her mouth was open so often she had her tonsils lagged. I haven't spoken to her for five years. It's not that we've had a row, it's just that I'm not quick enough to interrupt. When we're together, people think I'm a ventriloquist. Every time I open my mouth, she talks. It's obvious that she doesn't like me – she calls me effeminate. I don't mind because compared to her, I am.

MOVEN PIC SCRIPT   11

THANK YOU FOR THAT TRULY MAGNIFICENT RECEPTION LADIES &
GENTLEMEN - BECAUSE IF ITS TRUE THAT APPLAUSE BE
INDEED ~~the beautiful~~ MUSIC TO AN ARTISTS EARS THEN
ALL I'VE HEARD JUST LATELEY, IS "SILENT NIGHT"...
~~Rea lea~~ IT WAS SO BAD ON ONE OCCASION ~~when~~
TIME I WALKED OFF THE STAGE I GOT BOOKED
FOR LOITERING ~~whilst~~ ~~old lady in the front~~
~~ROW WAS told off for cleaning out~~
~~that was embarrassing enough but~~

script ideas

<u>Script seven</u>

<u>Neighbours</u>

Almost as important as the house you live in are your neighbours.
Mine are dreadful. When they're all together they look like a
pamphlet for Oxfam. The woman next door to me is is Welsh. Well,
I think she is, because the wife borrowed a cooking utensil from
her the other day and she came to the door and said, 'Can I have
my saucepan back?' And what a thin woman she is. I'm not
exaggerating, I've seen more fat on a cold chip. In her pyjamas, she
looks like latticework varicose veins. And talk about nosy, she said
to me the other day, 'The man across the road walks about the
house naked.' I said, 'You can't possibly see from your house.' She
said, 'You can if you lie on top of the wardrobe.' Her husband's
peculiar. He's only a little fellow, in fact, he wears turn-ups on his
underpants. Poor devil. Some men have bags under their eyes. He's
got his own left luggage office. Mind you, I'll say this for him he
wears the pants in his house. You can see them under his apron.

Korean
Rolex

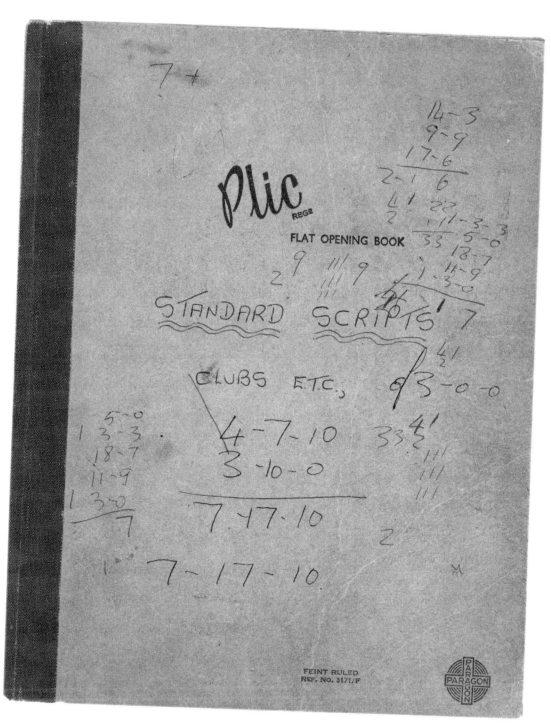

Plic REG2
FLAT OPENING BOOK

STANDARD SCRIPTS

CLUBS E.T.C.,

4 - 7 - 10
3 - 10 - 0
_____
7 - 17 - 10

7 - 17 - 10

FEINT RULED
REF. No. 3171/F

PARAGON

Script eight

The army and services

I see that the government is getting rid of more of the armed forces in an effort to save money. But don't worry. Even if war breaks out, we'll use a firm called Rent-a-Tank. Actually, although I've never mentioned it before, I come from a military family. It's not something I'm proud of. Well, you've heard of the thin red line? My family were the fat yellow streak. Whenever a war has broken out my family have been the first to go... and saw their trigger fingers off. One of my ancestors fought with Wellington – not the general, the boot. He shook so much they couldn't trust him with a gun. He ran away from the battle of Waterloo and got peppered with so many cannonballs, they didn't bury him, they weighed him for scrap. My great-grandfather went missing during the Boer War. They found him hiding in Baden Powell's hat. He got discharged on medical grounds. He'd had his hands up in the air so often they'd withered. My grandfather was a magnificient coward. During WWI, he had so many white feathers sent him, he played Oldham Empire for six years as Mother Goose.

But ~~sometimes~~ when you are at your lowest ebb and you find yourself wreathed in self pity something happens that makes you realise just how miniscule we are in the great scheme of creation...A fortnight ago(Full gag) ....Must put a roof on this lavatory. I did'nt know what to talk about this evening...I had pndered on the ~~idexxx~~ subject of my contribution to literature, but let's fa ce it, ~~ttxxxhxxtxxxxxxxblxxxxxxxxxxxxxxx~~ ~~xxtxxxxx~~ l am to writing books what Julie Andrews was to Deep Throat. So instead, l would like to **launch** on discourse regarding my career to date, a sort of potted ~~kxx~~ biog.

> ~~Rxxx~~ Go into: Name, not Les Dawson, chrotened Friday, when dad saw me he decided to call it a day.
>
> Ugly baby etc.
>
> Poor family etc.
> First love affair etc
> Marriage etc.

End on appeal.

SCRIPT.

(Orchestra plays bars of "Grand Opera")

"Our cat's got piles...I've always felt sorry for that cat, he was born in a bowler hat and he grew up roundshouldered.

For years 1 thought that cat only had one xxxx eye, then 1 found out it was walking backwards.

Over the years 1 have become an impassioned advocate for the preservation of wild life, that's why 1 want the wife's mother embalmed...before she dies.

There is a love that grows between man and beast, 1 saw a zoo keeper sobbing his heart out over the body of a dead elephant. 1 said you must have loved that creature very much. He said it's not that 1've got the bury the bloody thing.

My wofe had a narrow escape in a safari park recently, a lesser tufted Uganda baboon grabbed her in a very rampant fashion and started tearing her clothes off, she screamed what should 1 do 1 said do what you always do tell him you've got a headache.

<u>At The Straw Hat Club</u>

SCRIPT

In 1492, Christopher Columbus sailed across uncharted seas and despite scurvy, smallpox and a mutinous crew he went on to discover America and five years later he returned in triumph to Spain and his beloved Queen Isabella. In 1882, Stanley found Livingstone in the heart of the steaming Congo delta and together they returned from that green hell and their journey became an example of courage and heroism. In 1939, when he heard that war had broken out, my father went for a bottle of milk from the corner shop and we've never seen him since.

I seldom speak of my childhood. The trouble was I came as a shock to my parents. Mother was firmly convinced she was going into hospital to have a boil lanced and to make matters worse I was an incredibly ugly baby. Well, you can tell they had to give the midwife gas and air before she'd deliver me. The nurse held me up after the birth and said to Mother, 'Here's your son. Eight pounds.'

Mother looked at me and said, 'Make it nine-pounds-ten and I'll throw his cot in as well. I must have looked a mess because mother used to put me upside down in the trolley before she'd take me out. Its no wonder the neighbours thought I had fat cheeks and a cleft chin. When I blew a raspberry, I meant it.

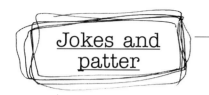

She's so fat that when she went to doctor for a check-up he said,
'I'll get the car out and have a look around you.'

☆☆☆☆

I wouldn't say the room was small but the fleas on the dog's
back didn't jump for fear of concussion.

☆☆☆☆

They say that time heals wounds,
but it caused most of mine.
The wife hit me with an alarm clock.

☆☆☆☆

I wouldn't say the house was damp but the kids went to bed
with a periscope.

☆☆☆☆

The service in restaurants gets worse.
I said to one waiter, 'Do I sit here until I starve?'
He said, 'No, we shut the kitchens at six.'

☆☆☆☆

Meat is so expensive where I live,
the wife doesn't go to a
butcher's, she goes to an auctioneer.

☆☆☆☆

When I auditioned for Bernard Delfont,
his cigar ash burnt my neck.
He couldn't help it, I was kissing his feet at the time.

☆☆☆☆

I'm not saying that our kitchen smells,
but we sometimes leave the gas on to clear the air.

☆☆☆☆

Kids are maturing so much earlier now.
Every Sunday I've been taking my six-year-old over
to the park to play on the swings and the slides.
Last Sunday he refused to go.
He said he's too old for that sort of thing.
So now I'll have to play on the swings on my own.

☆☆☆☆

I may look overwight but my doctor assures me that
for my age, I'm exactly the right weight –
though I should be twelve inches taller.
So he put me on a diet. I can eat anything I want –
bread, potatoes, cake, anything.
But I mustn't swallow it.

☆☆☆☆

My father was in the horse artillery,
but the feed bag kept falling off his ears.

☆☆☆☆

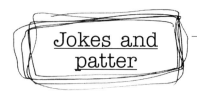

There was an old chap quite absurd
Who thought that he could fly like a bird
Watched by thousands of people
He leapt down from a steeple
He was buried on April the third

☆☆☆☆

The house is so cold we put the milk in the fridge
to stop it freezing.

☆☆☆☆

I said to the wife, 'I wish you wouldn't smoke in bed.'
She said, 'But a lot of women do.'
I said, 'Not bacon they don't.'

☆☆☆☆

When I was a lad my teeth stuck out so much,
Mother rented me out as a till.

☆☆☆☆

Ours is a football marriage,
we keep waiting for the other one to kick off.

☆☆☆☆

I stood entranced as he lightly fingered his crotchets.
He turned and when he saw me,
he whispered, 'It's Schubert.'
I said, 'It isn't, I smelt it when I came in.'

☆☆☆☆

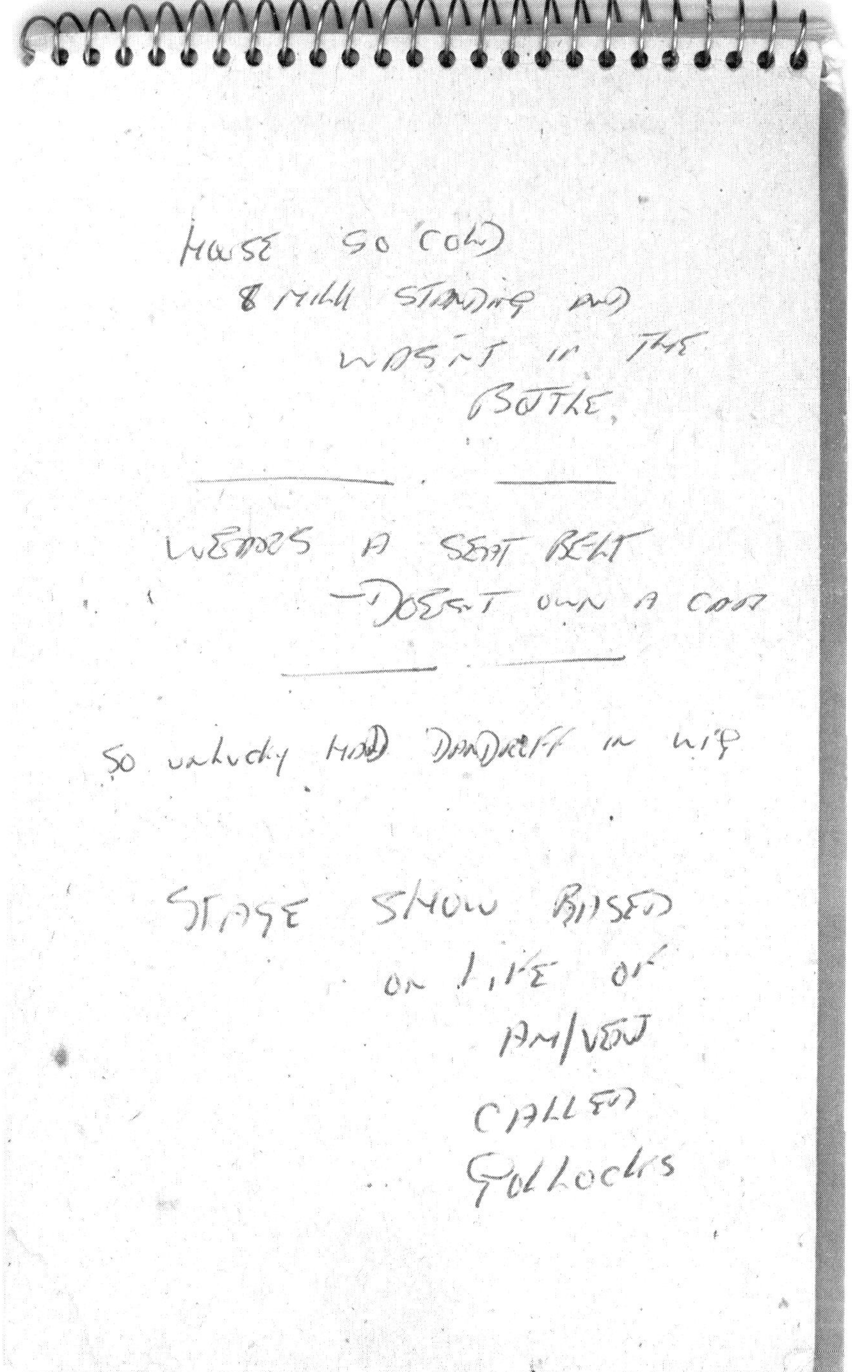

HOUSE 50 (OH)
8 MILL STANDING AND
WASN'T IN THE
BOTTLE.

_____

WEARS A SEAT BELT
→ DOESN'T OWN A CAR

_____

SO UNLUCKY HAD DANDRUFF IN WIG

STAGE SHOW BASED
ON LIFE OF
PM/VOW
CALLED
Pollocks

143

Ah, those stolen hours, when she would sit on my knee and lick my face all over. I said to her, 'Do you do that because you love me?' She said, 'No, I need the salt.' She said to me once in the rock garden where we used to get stoned together, 'What can I do about crow's feet?' I said, 'Wear socks.' And she whispered one night to me, 'If you die before me, I'll make sure everybody looks up to you.' I said, 'How?' She said, 'I'll bury you in a tree.' But it's the simple things I remember about her. The way she'd go to bed with a tape measure to see how long she'd slept.

⊥ took her out for a Chinese meal the other night, the waiter came over he said to her what you want...She said "Chicken" He said Chicken Atsoo...She said no ᵡᵡᵃᵃᵢᵡᵃᵡ l'll have a wing....ᴬᵡᵲᵲᵡShe really is ignorant, a fellow ᵏᵢᵲᵲᵏᵃᵈᵡᵃᵢᵡᵢᵏᵃᵡᵈᵃᵃᵃᵲᵡᵢᵏᵃᵡᵃᵢᵏᵃᵲᵡᵡᵃᵃᵲᵏᵡᵢᵃᵲᵡᵃᵃᵢᵈᵡᵡᵡ called to the house the other day he said l'm collecting for ᵢᵃᵲᵈ Lord Derby's trust fund the wife said l did'nt know he was ruptured... ᵏᶠᵡᵧᵃᵃᵢᵢᵲᵡᵲᵃᵢᵲᵲᵡᵲᵃᵃᵡᵧᵡᵲᵢᵲᵏᵡᵢᵏᵃᵢᵢᵡᵢᵢᵲᵧᵡᵢᵃᵲᵈᵡᵢᵃᵡᵈᵃᵃᵲᵲᵢᵏᵃᵡᵢᵃᵲ... ᵢᵃᵢᵏᵡᶠᵃᵲᵲᵃᵲᵲᵢᵃᵲᵢᵲᵡᵢᵢᵲᵃᵲᵃᵲᵃᵢᵲᵢᵲᵲᵃᶠᵡᵃᵢᵲᵲᵢᵲᵧᵡᵢᵲᵃᵡᵈᵃᵲᵲᵡᵲᵃᵲᵲᵢᵃᵲᵡᵢᵃᵲᵲᵢᵲ ᵢᵃᵡᵢᵃᵲᵡᵈᵲᵃᵡᵃᵲᵲᵡᵢᵲᵃᵡᵂᵢᵃᵢᵏᵡᵲᵃᵢᵢᵡᵡᵡᵲᵢᵃᵲᵲᵲᵃᵲᵲᵃᵡᶠᵃᵢᵡᵢᵃᵲᵃ
ᴵᵃ̸xx I've never forgotten our wedding day, the rays of the hot August sun filtered through the stained glass windows of the Medieval church highlighting the mellow antiguity of the saxon altar, and glinting on her father's rifle...ᵢᵢᵡᵂᵃᵲᵲᵃᵲᵃᵂᵢᵢᵲᵃᵡᵃᵲᵢᵢᵂᵃᵢᵢᵏᵡᵂᵃᵢᵏᵃᵈᵡᵈᵃᵃᵂᵡᵢᵃᵲᵲᵂᵃᵢᵏᵢᵃᵈ the ᵂᵢᶠᵃ organist was playing o perfect love til he saw the wife's family cantor down the aisle then he ᵲᵲᵃᵏᵃᵡᵢᵢᵲᵡᵏᵢᵃᵡᵢᵃᵲᵏᵡᵲᵃᵡᵗbroke into the march of the gladiators...We stood at the altar, the vicar took one look at the size of the wife, looked at me and ᵲᵢᵡ said do you take this woman or will you have her delivered...ᴮᵃᵲᵃᵲᵲᵲᵃᵲᵲᵃᵲᵃᵲᵃᵲᵏᵢᵢᵲᵃ̸ᵃ̸f don't get me wrong, l'm not saying the wife's fat, but when she stands in the garden in her vest, it looks ᵃᵃᵲᵢᶠ like a painting of an abbotoir... Still it could be worse we have three lovely children one of each... and we have been man and wife for over fifteen years and everywhere we go ᵂᵃ̸ still hold hands if we ever let go we'll kill one another....Tonight let us all forget the trappings of illusion get away from all this ill lit dross, and go back to the days when we all sat around the piano and ᵈ̸ang the old songs....Starting with.......

Cosmo Smallpiece was, actually, a great favourite of the ladies.

As you know, tonight is the anniversary of the death of one of Britain's great composers. I refer, of course, to Makepiece Twaddle.

He fell in love with a missionary's daughter from Bradford. He met her in a travel agency – she was looking for a holiday and he was the last resort. It wasn't a happy marriage. She was so fat, she got her knickers on a prescription and she was so bow-legged she hung her stockings on a boomerang. It ended in disaster. One night she fell asleep on a water bed and the house set on fire and she was poached to death. It was at this time that Makepiece Twaddle wrote a hit song about a tom cat that bit Edmund Purdom the actor, it was called 'Purdom me, Boy, Is that the Cat you Knew that Chewed You?'.

○ ○ ○○

'As Time Goes By'. Strange how a snatch of song can rekindle the embers of an old memory. Wise men say that time heals all things but time alone can never dull the ache I still feel when I recall my first love affair – nor can time ever erase the scars of passion that are etched on my heart.

Even now, all these years later, jumbled images of the past jostle with sight and sound to evoke the old yearnings.

Rain sweeping along the boulevard of Saint Germain in Paris... Cafe windows in Istanbul streaked with condensation, distorting lovers on the Galata Bridge... Sunlight shimmering into patterns on Lake Geneva... A plumber's hut on a building site in Rhyl... Yes, they are all part of the affair. Many women have travelled the road to immortality – Helen of Troy, Cleopatra of the Nile. Add then to that illustrious list the name Gladys Pickledick of Oldham. When I met her for the first time, I wasn't in showbusiness, I was working as a meat pie reviver for British Railways. I was on sick leave at the time, I'd been attacked in a buffet at Crewe by a grapefruit cocktail. Grapefruits are vicious – stick a spoon in them and they go for the eyes. Gladys was a caretaker of a karate school. The wages were lousy but she got plenty of backhanders.

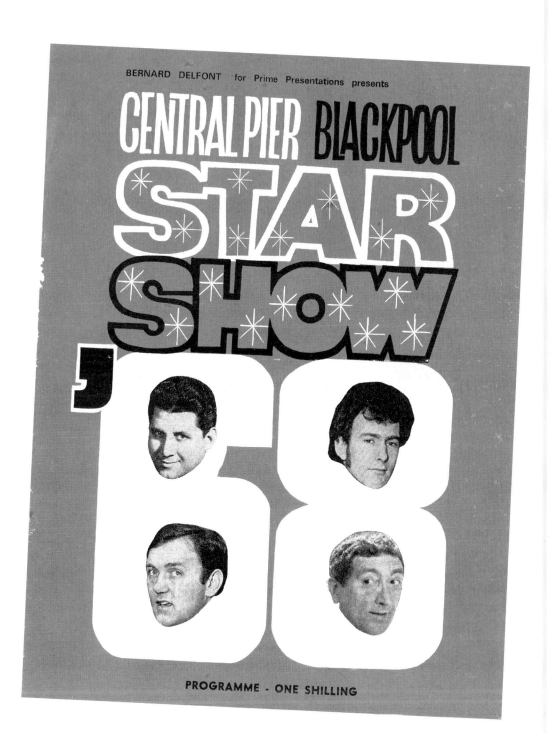

BERNARD DELFONT for Prime Presentations presents

CENTRAL PIER BLACKPOOL
STAR SHOW '68

PROGRAMME · ONE SHILLING

Many ills beset mankind. Famine, pestilence and plague go hand-in-hand with the evil drummers of war and intolerance that threaten to march humanity to the very edge of armageddon. And yet, there is a greater horror than even these – its name is marriage.

There can be nothing more dreadful than the average English wedding. Last week, much against my will, I attended the marriage ceremony of the wife's eldest sister, Gertrude. Now, there's a woman for you... I think. She's so big and fat, as she walked down the aisle in her white wedding dress, you got the impression of someone towing a sight screen at Lord's. She's so vast, she doesn't have a bath, we hose her down in the yard. She went for a swim in the nude once and you could hear the coastguard shout, 'Tha' she blows!' I'm not for one moment saying that she's ugly, but when she went to have a tooth out, the dentist took one look at her face and worked through her chest.

I felt sorry for the bridegroom. He was wearing a hired suit of tails. I'm not saying he looked a mess, but Moss Brothers were picketing the church and I don't think I've seen a thinner man. In those tails, he looked like a penguin who's overdone it at WeightWatchers.

As they stood at the altar the vicar took one look at them and asked if it was *Candid Camera*. The choir boys went pale at the sight and the organist gave them binkers. The mother-in-law was there. She was dressed in a white coat, black gloves and shoes and she had so much makeup on she looked like a giant panda with dropsy. It was obvious that she was glad to get rid of her daughter because she didn't have a bunch of flowers in her lapel, she was waving a football rattle. The father-in-law was, as per usual, the worse for drink. Every time he yawned, he lit the altar candles. Mercifully, the ghastly ceremony was at last over, after the bridegroom managed to get the ring on her finger with the help of some Vaseline and a tyre lever and, as the poor idiot kissed her, the vicar shouted, 'It's not too late, my son, you can demand sanctuary.'

At the reception, both families sat as far away from each other as was humanly possible. The catering was awful. The wife threw a chicken leg to a dog, who chewed for an hour then spent the rest of the night with his paw down to its throat. God, it was terrible. There was a three-piece band – a pianist, his fingers and a stool. He played three songs then went to pieces. The best man sang a dirty song and was sick down my uncle's ear trumpet. The bridegroom's father called the wife's mother a rancid old bag and his face lit up. She'd pushed his nose up a lamp socket. Some fool fell asleep in the loo and before long we were all doing the twist.

Soon it was all over and the happy couple lumbered off on their honeymoon. They were going on a P&O cruise – pubs and off licences. It wasn't a very romantic honeymoon. Gertrude turned out to be frigid and the doctor gave the bridegroom some tablets to make her passionate. To prove there was nothing wrong with them he took one too. That night, apparently, she woke up and said, 'Ooh I do fancy a man,' and he said, 'That's funny... so do I.'

SAID TO WIFE FANCY
HAVING SEX LIKE DOGS
YES PROVIDING WE DO IT
IN A STREET WHERE THEY
DON'T KNOW US

T.V. OLD — HAS STARTING HANDLE.

BEAUTY CLINIC USED TO RICKET MY PRAM.

FEET SO BIG ~~JEAN~~ SHE'S A
MARKER FOR MOTORWAYS.

CHIROPODISTS ON SHIFT WORK

PUSH WHEN EAT FISH WEAR YACHTING
CAPS.

DONT SAY CREAMY CRACKER — CREME DE
CRACKER.

WHERE THEY PUT SILENCERS ON THE
TOILET CHAINS

KICK START BOWINGS.

My wife sent her photograph to a lonely heart's club.
They sent it back and said they weren't that lonely.

☆☆☆☆

I wouldn't say she was fat but when she wants a dress
she goes to a quantity surveyor.

☆☆☆☆

I wouldn't say the plane was old but they didn't say,
'Fasten your safety belts', they shouted,
'Buckle your breast plates.'

☆☆☆☆

What amazes me is that so many people think showbusiness
is glamorous and exciting.
Believe me, it's about as glamorous as changing sheets
in a bed-wetting clinic.

☆☆☆☆

She was so ignorant,
she thought a millimetre was a Spanish earwig.

☆☆☆☆

I wouldn't say the room was small but
we used a folding toothbrush in the bathroom.

☆☆☆☆

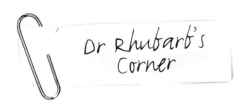

Les's radio show featured helpful hints from his agony uncle Dr Rhubarb.

Dr Rhubarb's Corner

Daphne: Time now for listeners' problems to be answered by our resident professor of philosophy and psychology, Dr Armitage Rhubarb, MD, PhD, PTO and ABC.

Question: My husband sleeps all day in a box and he goes out a lot at night with his hair plastered down and a cape on. We've not been married long and I think he's peculiar. He gets on well with bats and he keeps biting my neck. Mother likes him but she's very pale and doesn't say a lot. There's no room for me in his box and the soil gets in my tights. Where has our marriage gone wrong?

Answer: There's nothing wrong with your marriage. He's going through a male menopause by the sound of it. Make him a member of a blood bank and throw him the odd piece of fillet. If he likes a drink, let him go out, but don't let him bite a dwarf's neck, because I should imagine he could get nasty if he drinks shorts.

Dr Rhubarb's Corner

Once again, for those with a problem help is at hand with Dr Rhubarb's Corner.

Question: I'm a German egg hynotist and quite tall in winter. I own an off licence and a month ago my cocker spaniel fell down a culvert and died. I loved that dog so much I cut his tail off and hung it above a bottle of rum. The other night while I was ironing my son's piano accordion my ears began to ring and when I answered them it was a wrong number. Just then the ghost of my cocker spaniel materi alised from a bottle of pickles and asked for his tail back. I was frightened and I couldn't get my teeth out of a mince pie. Should I have given the dog his tail back? I didn't know what to do because it was after midnight. I lost my husband a year ago. He's not dead, I just lost him. Help me.

Answer: You did right not to give the ghost of your dog his tail back. It would have got you into trouble with the police because, as you well know, you're not allowed to retail spirits after 10.30pm.

Dr Rhubarb's Corner.

Time now for listeners problems to be answered and their troubles eased
by that eminent humanist, Dr Rhubarb, in the part of the programme we call
: Dr Rhubarb's Corner.

Question from puzzled of Barnolds wick:

"My eldest son was having a shave last week when he noticed he was
changing into a horse. Since then he's bought himself a saddle
and he's eate the window box. My husband can't understand what's
happening and he's walled himself up in the attic. My son who has
three "O" levels and plays ragtime on a bugle, now sleeps stood up
in the kitchen and waits for the milkman to give him sugar.
He won't go on a bus so can you come to our house and have a word with
him"

Answer: Dear Puzzled...Don't fret too much and keep away from his teeth.
You'll save on school uniforms and socks but for modesty's sake
let him wear a pair of shorts or a kilt , 1 had a patient who turned
into a buffalo and he was looked after by a billygoat, well he could'nt
afford a nanny. Now 1 canT get round to your house to see you son, so
this is what 1 suggest. give him a big meat of braised oats and
prune juice, then bring him to my surgery and 1'll talk to him
provideing he walks over my roses. P.S can you bring a shovel

. . .

Question(Baffled of Ealing) "Six weeks ago 1 found that a pimple on my nose
had turned into a thatched cottage with an orchard. How strange
said my mistress who is a. Veitnamese welder. Imagine my surprise
when on the following morning, there was a small river running from
the cottage on my nose to my left ear, and on top of the bridge of
my nose just behind the chimney, 1 saw a clump of dwarf gladioli
leading to a lawn on my cheek. Even as 1 write to you
a bunch of lupins are growing on my lip. is this unusual? I'm
not forty yet and do yoga...Advice please...I'm worried

Answer: Don't be wrried, you've got a beauty spot.

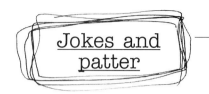

Robin and his merry men they frolic in the sun
And if you ask, 'Who's Maid Marion?'
They answer, 'Everyone.'

He said, 'I were watching your act from behind the snooker table.
Are you approachable?'
I said, 'Yes.' He said, 'Can I give you a word of
constructive criticism?' I said, 'Certainly.'
He said, 'I think you're crap.'

☆☆☆☆

The house is so damp, the gas meter's full of
octopus droppings.

☆☆☆☆

A friend of mine had a cousin called Sam,
a fat fellow who owned a disco in San Francisco.
My friend went to visit him and he drove to 'Frisco
in a rented hearse.
He had a great time and then found that he'd lost the hearse.
It wasn't until three days later he remembered
where he'd mislaid it and he sang:
'Ivor left my hearse in fat Sam's disco.'

☆☆☆☆

We hadn't a telly.
We used to sit and watch the fire go out.
Then we'd go and order another shovelful of coal.

☆☆☆☆

Les on... money

Nothing's gone right just lately, I got a letter from the bank the other day. I wasn't surprised. The last time I put money in our joint account, they were talking about home rule for Vikings. I went to the bank last Friday.

I said to the bank manager, 'How does my account stand?' and he said, 'I'll toss you for it.' We sat down in his office. He said, 'Before I discuss a loan, Mr Dawson, I must ask you – have you got collateral?' I said, 'No, it's the way my legs are crossed.'

He said, 'You've been coming here for seven years and in all that time you have never noticed that I've got a glass eye.'

I said, 'I have – it's your left one.' He said, 'How did you know?'

I said, 'It's the only one with a spark of humanity in it.' I didn't get a loan. I didn't really expect one. That bank manager is so mean he swims under toll bridges. He learned Braille so he could read in bed with the light off.

Still we've all got problems. I've got one with the house I've just bought. It was a dream house – I must have been asleep when I bought it. It's so jerry built that if they ever demolish it for slum clearance they'll have to repair it first before it's safe to pull down. I saw it advertised by an estate agent. You know the way they make it sound – it said: 'For sale mod con sem det dub gag fit kit exel gads rur asp cen heat.'

I said, 'How much do you want for the mod con sem det tach dub gag fit kit exel gads rur asp cen heat?'

He said, 'Two thou fif hun nun puns.' I got it for sixteen-fifty. I think that was the year it was built. It's so damp, when we set a mouse trap we catch an otter. We don't have bedbugs, the kids are full of whelk bites. I got on the phone to the surveyor. I said, 'I want the house pointing.' He said, 'Certainly. Which way?'

○ ○ ○○

A famous philosopher once remarked that the sound of an audience laughing was like heavy rain falling onto a placid lake and that applause was the noise of a river rushing to the sea. If what he said was true then the best way to describe my act is a sort of do-it-yourself drought kit...

○ ○ ○○

But it is a great pleasure to be on this wonderful programme before such a wonderful audience and to see again the ever wonderful Val Doonican. And that's one thing you'll find about me, I may be a lousy comic but I'm the biggest creep in the show. It's a case of having to be because financially things are getting worse... And I'm so far behind with my mortgage repayments now the arrears are ticked off in the Doomesday Book... I can't seem to save a penny these days. The last time I put money in my bank account the song at the top of the hit parade was 'Greensleeves'.

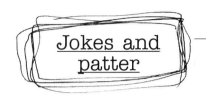

Jokes and patter

I wouldn't say the ship was old but ...

THE CREW DIDN'T DO THE HORN-PIPE - THEY
DANCED THE MINUET

•

ITS ANCHOR WAS CROWNED AND CAPPED

•

SOMEBODY HAD WRITTEN ON THE CABIN WALL:
"GO HOME ROMANS"

•

THEY GOT THE DECKS FITTED ON THE
NATIONAL HEALTH

•

THE SHIP WAS INSURED AGAINST FIRE AND
WITCHCRAFT

•

THE SHIP'S LOG WAS WRITTEN IN LATIN

•

IT HAD A STARTING HANDLE

I wouldn't say she was fat
but the WeightWatchers wore blinkers.

☆☆☆☆

We were so poor,
after the flag seller had called,
we had to fire a distress rocket.

☆☆☆☆

If success breeds success,
then I must be on the pill.

☆☆☆☆

No laughs hey? I know the act smells,
but I'm right on top of it and you don't hear me complain.

☆☆☆☆

What a wonderful ovation.
After that, I can hardly wait to hear what
I'm going to say.

☆☆☆☆

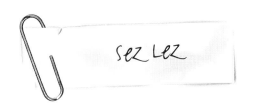

While producer John Duncan and Les were backstage at a theatre thinking of titles for a new show, a gorgeous young dancer came by. Bantering with Les, she jokingly finished with, 'We don't take any notice of what Les says.' Sez Les ran for eight years and made him an established star.

Sez Lez

Spot

[WITH CHOIR AND MUSIC: 'GREENSLEEVES']

I fled the garish neon jungle we call city and wandered through the rolling sanctum of the Cotswolds. I found myself in a valley of timeless serenity, of yawning meadows and stately forests within whose beckoning greenery feathered choristers trilled on high. It was all too much and I stretched myself by a chuckling brook and sobbed my self-pity into a dreamless sleep. I awoke and found a rosy-cheeked old lady bending over my prostate form with concern etched in her old eyes. She led me to a Tudor cottage that groaned with the weight of antiquity on its black and white timbers. She bade me enter the warm glow and I thanked her for her desire to help me. What a grand lady she was. She trusted every living creature. She didn't bother to lock the doors of the cottage. Indeed, there wasn't even a lock on the outside toilet. When I mentioned this fact, she looked at me astonished and said, 'There's not been a lock on the toilet door for over forty years and nobody's pinched the bucket yet...'

...SPOT SEVEN...SEZ LES...

SING: "THAT'S LIFE"

One thing is sure in life and that is everything has to come to an end...This show is the last in the present series and l've enjoyed every pay check of it...mind you l'm not in this business just for the money...and thats the truth...if its not then may the Gods strike me speechless for saying it..no....(Silence)

lts been a pleasure to come to Yorkshire television..the studios here are just like home...filthy and full of strangers...everybody here works together like brothers, the Kray Brothers..lts been great meeting old friends like Syd Lawrence and his old moore's almanack. the orchestra that has put the big band sound firmly back..on its back...Sucess has'nt altered Syd...he's still as sickening as ever... He's done very well for himself, he's got a Rolls Royce, and he's going into the coffee business so that he can have a nouse in its own grounds. He has a telephone in his bedroom it does'nt ring..it claps...Last week the band played at the Bisley Rifle Club's annual hot pot supper and after the show Syd was presented with six silver bullets inscibed, nobody knows what's written on them because they have'nt been dug out of his chest yet...Despite~his~advanced~age~just~still~play~that~ trumpet~   Despite his advanced age just wait until you hear Syd play that trumpet...l'm not saying its a loud noise but they're re-pointing the walls at Jericho...Its been xxjm an ex perience working with our new producer...we got him cheap, not surprising really because on the last show he produced, Henry Hall was the guest...He's been on the dole so often when they build a new labour exchange they call him in as a consultant...ixwxxxamxxexxwhenxlxfixexxsawxhim..hexxxxxwexxingxxxyexlex xaxdigxnyxxxellexxxtxemearexxandxhixxnxixxwaxxbackxcombexxyhexxxmkexxxlxx xxxarxxxhyxxxxxexixhxmxayxlxxxxidxxexxmexfellxwxxx lxxxixxxpxxexxtimexnexxaxbigxgamexhuntexxxxlxxxidxxmxtxxxxxzhexbiggextx xxxxxlxxxxxthxtxyxmxxexexxxmexxxfxxxxxxlnexxxidxitxxxxxtnexx

28 SHEETS RULED

SEZ LES

LI⊙N BRAND

Script

WHITE VELLUM

A John Dickinson Product

162

Les Dawson SHOW . ONE 1

OPENING AS WRITTEN: THEN INTO "SEZ LES"
WALK DOWN THROUGH ORCHESTRA AND DANCE ROUTINE
(WITH LETTERS?) RUNNERS CLOSE AND INTO PATTER.

(PATTER   MATERIAL)

END OF PATTER BECKON CAMERA AND TRACK THRO'
INTO SET WHICH IS SAME AS THE OPENING BUT
NOW THE DANCERS ARE GOING IN A SHORT VERSION
OF PERHAPS "AMERICAN IN PARIS" - GIVES LES TIME TO
CHANGE FOR AN APACHE ROUTINE WITH LARGE WOMAN
WHO THROWS HIM OUT OF SHOT - LOUD CRASH
AND "TALKING PIANO" LAUGHS AND SAYS "GIVE THAT
WOMAN A SERIES". - DANCERS GO INTO THE "CAN CAN"
ROUTINE - CUT TO COSMO AT A TABLE (HOOKED OFF)
SHOT OF W.C FIELDS SAYING TO WAITER "

<u>Sez Lez</u>

January
<u>Script one 'Lonesome Rhodes'</u>

[SING: 'OH GIVE ME A HOME WHERE THE BUFFALO ROAM AND YOU'LL ALWAYS HAVE A DEEP PILE ON YOUR CARPET']
[SING: 'I WOKE UP THIS MORNING WHEN THE SUN DIDN'T SHINE, I PICKED UP MY SHOVEL AND WENT TO THE MINE. I LOADED SIXTEEN TONS OF NUMBER NINE COAL... AND GOT A HERNIA']

Howdy partners.. [THROW GUN] Yeah, I'm a gun slinger. My name is Lonesome Rhodes. Folks keep well away from me. I've got two guns, a hot temper and BO. I'm the fastest draw in the West. You don't believe me? Well, watch... Want to see it again?

I played my part in taming the Wild West. It was me who cleaned up the one horse town of Dodge. It wasn't easy, I only had a small shovel. It was a dangerous job. One day I pulled up my cart with a jerk, my load of manure was insecure, and I was up to my neck in my work.

I was born with a guitar and a shotgun on my knee. It was a hell of a job getting my trousers on. My family were called the bicarbonates because they were early settlers. My grandpappy was an old Indian fighter. That's what he married, an old Indian. She was so fat, when she went down in Sacramento, they had an eclipse in Bournemouth.

Grandpappy had a factory that made earrings for red indians. It was a sort of Injun-earring works. That's what we call a wagon train joke – every time I tell it, it goes west. My mother was the daughter of a sewage works inspector but she was nothing to be sniffed at. She was so small her drawers were soled and heeled. Every time she pulled her stockings up, her garters stung her ears. And she was so thin that when a fire broke out in a hairdressing salon, she escaped through a Carmen roller. She was the only woman I know who padded out her lipstick. My daddy bred prize bulls and shipped then all over the world. He was the biggest bull-shipper in the west.

In one pitched battle with the Indians he had over a hundred arrows in his back but lived for ten years to tell the tale, then died of woodworm. As I cradled his head in my arms and gave him a spoonful of Rentokil, I said, 'Who did it, paw? Blackfeet?' He said, 'I don't know, son, but their necks were filthy.' I was madder than a rattlesnake at a cup final. I took my horse down off a clothes peg – it's always on a clothes peg because it's a mustang. It's a beautiful animal. The only trouble is I can only go backwards. It's a sort of clop clip every trip.

That night I rode into Tombstone and sprained my ankle on it. I never saw it because it was so foggy. I tried whistling for a taxi twice and couldn't find my lips. Just then a bald Indian came over, so I sold him a hot poultice to keep his wig warm. He said, 'You come now to teepee?' and I said, 'With pleasure,' because I was dying to go. In fact, I'd crossed my legs so often on the trail I'd plaited my truss. Those darn redskins kept jabbing me with spears and offering my blood to the Gods. I had to escape, I was sick of being stuck for the drinks. Gotta go now, it's the bread festival in Texas. They throw a loaf in the air and you have to watch a slice. Most of the loaf will be gone but I'm hoping to get there in time for the last round up.

Sez Lez

Christmas

[SING: 'SHAKE HANDS WITH A MILLIONAIRE']

My father. He'd been out of work so long his insurance stamps had Caesar's head on them. He only married my mother because she agreed to have the ceremony in a chapel of rest. I said to him once, 'Why don't you get out of bed and a have a walk round outside?' He said, 'Listen, son. Opportunity only knocks once and I want to be in when it calls.'

Show four

Spot

The wife and I had an early holiday this year. We went in February on a cheap ten-day cruise. You could tell it was cheap cruise – gun boats kept cutting our nets. It was a terrible trip. God knows how old the ship was we went on, but they started it with a whip. It's the only one I've ever seen with a thatched funnel. Business was so bad they were advertising for hijackers. I didn't like the captain, he kept tripping me up with his crutch and his parrot bit me. I don't know how long he'd been at sea, but he didn't have piles, he had barnacle rash.

My missus made a fool of herself. She kept walking about in a bikini. You can tell what she looked like – the crew were flirting with me. She's not got the figure for a bikini. I'm not saying she's fat, but she used to be a decoy with a whaling feet. She stood in the garden once with her vest and the neighbours thought we'd painted the house. Mind you, she once lost two stone swimming in a canal. I couldn't understand it – I'd tied them round her neck tight enough.

The food on the ship was awful. It was so bad, seagulls used to swoop down and drop Red Cross parcels. The meals were supposed to be cordon bleu – in my opinion they should have been cordoned off. One night I had roast pigeon. I don't know how long it had been in the kitchen but strapped to its leg was an SOS from the *Titanic*. It didn't put the wife off though. She ate everything before her and her table manners leave a lot to be desired. Every time she drank soup a sailor would stand up and shout, 'Abandon ship!' What a noise – it sounded like somebody flushing a reservoir. I've never known a woman eat so fast. At home she sets the table with a jockey's blouse and we've got spark plugs on the cruet. One night on the ship she had six bread rolls, four extra portions of chips and three peach melbas. The wine waiter said, 'What would madam like to wash it down with?' I said, 'I'm not sure but try the Bay of Biscay.' She's no idea of social graces. One day at the bar the waiter said, 'Would you like an aperitif?' She said, 'No, my own dentures are good enough.'

There wasn't much entertainment on the ship. They had a film show every night.

It was the same film. I didn't mind, I quite got to like Mary Pickford. During the day we played games like hunt the mutineers and guessing the speed of the rats jumping over the side. There was a cabaret twice a week – it was Ronnie Ronalde whistling for the wind.

We finally docked in Portugal. The weather was shocking. It was so cold, the sardines were oiling themselves. We finished up putting anti-freeze in the suntan lotion. Mind you, it only rained three times – morning, noon and night. One fellow came back on board with a case of dysentery. The wife said, 'Well at least it'll make a change from lager.'

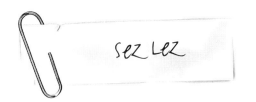
sez Les

Spot

[WITH MUSIC AND CHOIR: 'A STRANGER ON THE SHORE']

In 1886, my great great grandfather, the Very Reverend Uriah Dawson, who was known locally as the randy resurrectionist, fled his parish in Ormskirk after a scandal involving a brigadier in a tattoo parlour. Disguised as a ship's chandler, he sailed to Canada and became a beaver breeder and bingo caller in Winnipeg. The wanderlust overtook him and he trekked north to the wild lands where, armed only with his musket, he faced the hostility of nature. One day he was caught in a blizzard in Mackenzie Sound and before long he was fighting for every breath he drew. Ice particles formed on his eyelids and his hand was frozen on his fowling piece. He cried hoarsely as he lurched through the swirling snow and the biting, bitter wind and he lay down to await the coming of the grim reaper. At that moment, an Indian maiden who was stood on the other side of a huge lake called softly, 'Do not die, oh great white hunter, for I love you.' It gave him renewed will to live, so he burrowed a hole in the ice field and lived on the odd titmouse and ice patties. When spring came and the great thaw took place, he took to standing on his side of the lake and shouting across, 'I love you.' And she would shout back from her side, 'I love you.' He couldn't get across because the lake was always cold and partly frozen. He plunged in and stiff as a piece of three-ply... Indians never forgot what he did, named lake after him... Lake Stupid.

...SHOW FIVE SPOT FIVE SEZ LES...

But one way or another last week did'nt go well at all..if On Monday l tried to
sell my house, l put it in the hands of an estate agent, he made it sound so nice
l went out and bought it again...One fellow came to see it, he looked round and said
I'm afraid this is not the sort of thing I'm looking for at all...too small by far,
he said my othe house was a neo gothic manor house in its own five acres of lawns
and orchards, my staircase was a hint of Georgian and the oak panelled library
ran into a majestic booklined Jacobean study with mullioned windows that overlooked
the tennis courts and the Saxon battlements on the west wing tower, two stone
heraldic beasts sat in contemplation of the ornamental lake and the servants quarter
which squat near the archway to the maze and the marble patio...l said it sounds
marvellous, why did you leave it...he said it fell down...
On Tuesday the mother - in - lwas came up, l knew it was her knocking because the
  wood worm xxxxx came out and begged for rent o kil....and the flies in the kitchen
were swatting one another.She did'nt look to good apparently she'd wrenched her
  shoulder in Scotland tossing the caber...She's a big woman...she gets her brassiere
fitted on by "impeys.... The wife said have you put the gas fire on in my mother s
room, l said yes but l have'nt lit it...mind you the mother in law makes it xxxxix
obvious that she does'nt like me, when it was my birthday she bought me a celloloid
nightshirt and a xxxxix faulty candle...
On Wednesday night l had trouble with the next door neighbours...three o clock in th
morning they were shouting screaming and banging on the walls...luckily l was'nt
asleep, l was playing my drums at the time...theyxtrexxxfunnyxexxplex we ve got some
rum looking neighbours, fellow across the road is so bald everytime he goesto a
bowling alley people put their fingers up his nose..two flies were walking across
his head the other day one said its amazing how things change, when l was your age
this was a footpath...xki Thursday night l went into our local pub its called the
"Dumb Fortnight ..because the beer's too weak for words..l've never tasted beer
like it its so flat its served in an envelope... l was stood at the bar and a drunke
xxii little fellow teekxx tried to pinch my pint so l knocked him to the floor with
a karate chop to the neck..half an hour later he came back stood on a chair and
belted me with a stiff right arm jab..when l came too l said what sort of a blow
was that, he shoved his coat sleeve up and said a nineteen thirty five morris
starting handle...twxxbxathxxxxgxxixxxthxixpubxxxlfxxxdxxxxxxx osu then a fellow
came in, landlord said hello Alfred have'nt seen you for a while..(Full gag:
  Quick as a flash...RASP)

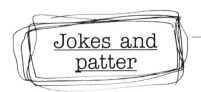

Jokes and patter

A lot of people firmly believe that showbusiness
consists of all-night parties
and sex orgies.
Well, the nearest I've been to an orgy
was when the au pair's garters
snapped at Scrabble.

☆☆☆☆

You might not know this, but I started my career
singing in the streets.
I was so bad,
they threw me into the nearest theatre.

☆☆☆☆

But I'm still so poor,
if I wrote a blank cheque,
it would bounce.

☆☆☆☆

I wouldn't say they were posh but the toilet coughed
before it flushed.

☆☆☆☆

He was the only comic to have been thrown out of places
he hasn't even worked at.

☆☆☆☆

There's so much squalor in our town that the Lord Mayor
suggests that we make the fungus our national flower.

☆☆☆☆

Les in the Les Dawson Golf Classic at Lytham.

Monologue

Well, they knocked me down, beat me, kicked me and robbed me, so I went to learn karate. You know what karate is, don't you? That's where you break a piece of wood with your bare hands. That's very useful because if anyone attacks you after that, you've got two pieces of wood to hit them with.

Karate is like yoga, it's all psychological. But I took lessons and I was very good at it. On the first day I managed to break one board. [MIME CHOPPING BOARD WITH SIDE OF HAND] The second day I did much better, I broke four boards, with the plaster case I was wearing from the first day.

It was the Japanese who invented karate and they do it right. They scream before they hit the wood. [DEMONSTRATE BY DOING JAPANESE SCREAM THEN MIME CHOPPING WOOD. THEN DO IT OTHER WAY ROUND. MIME CHOPPING WOOD AND THEN SCREAM IN PAIN, HOLDING HAND]

The interesting thing about karate is that you can kill a man with your bare feet. I bumped into the same three robbers again one night and I thought to myself, 'This time I'll use karate, I'll cripple 'em with my feet.' But by the time I'd got my shoelace untied they'd beaten me up and robbed me again. I can chop a man in half with one hand, but with two hands I couldn't untie that knot in my shoelace. Now I don't take chances. Wherever I go now I carry a flick knife. And as soon as I see danger, I get the knife out of my pocket, flick open the blade... and cut my shoelaces.

The most important part of karate is the scream. You can scare away an attacker with just the scream. I do it so well I scare myself. One day I saw this giant of a man coming towards me. So right away I used my karate screams. [DO SCREAMS] But he still came towards me. So I screamed louder. [LOUDER KARATE SCREAMS] But he still kept coming. Just my luck – he was deaf! So I bought him a hearing aid.

If any of your people in the audience are thinking of taking up karate, let me give you a useful tip. There are times when the hand chop, the barefoot kick and the karate screams won't work. In cases like that I've developed a little trick of my own that always gets me out of trouble. Here's what you do. You clench your left fist and place it on your left hip. Clench your right fist and place it on your right hip. Raise your right knee up like this.

[DEMONSTRATE] Got that? Right. Now, as your attacker comes at you... you run for your life. Goodbye. [RUN OFF]

○ ○ ○ ○

The wife and I were on a tandem holiday in Wales. A wonderful experience, I got cramp in Caerphilly and a continuous ache in the Rhondda. One day I thought I'd gone deaf but I hadn't, the wife had fell off the bike. She lay sprawled in the buttercups with her backside humped in the air. And with her size she looked rather like a corduroy Mount Snowdon.

○ ○ ○ ○

I am of course an expert marksman, and one day a tiger chased me into a hole in a stone canyon, and sat waiting for me to come out, I only had one bullet in my gun. I knew that if fired at the stone wall, which was a foot away from me, the bullet would ricochet off the wall at an angle of thirty-five degrees, bounce off a boulder, ping off a tree in a trajectory of 4.3 in the ballisics scale, slice off the sand and enter the tiger's lumber tregion and render him hors de combat.

I suppose you're all wondering if I killed the tiger – no, I missed the wall.

I wouldn't say the show was lousy but it was such a cheap version
of *South Pacific* it was called *South Pathetic*.

I've tried so hard to get on – pubs, clubs, theatres,
they're all excellent sources of unemployment to me.

He asked me if I lived around here. I told him,
'Just along the road.' He asked what number. I told him,
'No number. Just along the road.'

I was lying in bed the other morning playing a lament
on my euphonium when the wife,
who was prising her teeth out of an apple,
looked at me and said softly, 'Joey.' She calls me Joey
because she always wanted a budgie.
She said: 'I'm homesick.'
I said, 'But, precious one, this is your home.' She said,
'I know, and I'm sick of it.'

I wouldn't say they were posh but the mice made
trap reservations.

Some years ago, a mystic swami came to live above a butcher's shop in a town in Scotland called Forfar. One Saturday he was refused admission to see the town's football team, Forfar Athletic, so he cast a curse on the team. And for the next two years, they never won at home matches.

One man fought the evil swami. His name was Eric Von Hertz, a German – at least, every time he went through a field of cows he would shout, 'Ach! Dung.' He found the best way to get rid of the curse was to burn feathers and hurl them towards a wooden gnome that the swami kept in the back garden.

All that was needed to complete the fight against the curse was for the butcher over whose shop the swami lived to cheat the evil swami by pressing down on the scales when the swami bought liver. This had to be done when Forfar had an away match.

Soon all was ready, Von Hertz set fire to the feathers and his wife phoned up the butcher and said, 'Get ready to cheat the swami with his liver.'

The butcher was nervous. 'Are you sure it will work? Are you sure your husband has lit the feathers?' And she replied:

'Weigh down upon the swami's liver, Forfar's away. I swear my Hertz is feather-burning thrown at the old oak gnome.'

○ ○ ○○

One day the chief gathered his possessions together and left to take up his new job as a Liberal MP in Bradford. As he was carried from the camp in a buffalo hide litter, an old squaw was singing her lament and cried to the chief: 'When you live in England find my son – his name's Hennywaninder and he lives in London, WC1. Tell him I grieve for him, my son.'

The chief was moved and when in London he walked through the West End and said to a policeman, 'Where's WC?' The policeman pointed to some toilets and the chief strode in. He saw a door marked 'WC one'. He banged on the door with his lance and shouted, 'Henny-wan-inder?' A voice said, 'Yes.' So the chief broke the door down and saw a little fellow sat there reading a copy of *Old Moore's Almanack*. He picked him up, hung him on a hook, twanged his braces and hit him with a machete. 'Now, in future write to your mother.'

Eric Sykes, Les and Peter Goodwright travelling in style.

Here Les goes through the various permutations of one of his tangled musical puns, worked around the words of the song 'If you ever go across the sea to Ireland'.

DURING MY TOUR OF THE FAR EAST I SPENT SOME TIME IN THAILAND A BEAUTIFUL COUNTRY THAT UNFORTUNATELY HAS A PROBLEM WITH ANIMALS APPARENTLY YOUNG COWS - WHICH ARE OF COURSE CALLED HEIFERS TEND TO GNAW GOATS ITS DUE TO THE HAY BEING FRAYED AT THE ENDS - WHILE I WAS THERE I MET A MAN CALLED GORDON WHO HAD TWO HUNDRED MOORHENS AND HE LET THEM RACE ACROSS HIS LEGS - AND IT WAS QUITE A SIGHT TO SIT THERE AND WATCH THE BIRDS RUN OVER HIM GORDON'S SON WAS A SCIENTIST WHO WAS TRYING TO GROW DOWN ON GELDED BAY HORSES — IT WAS MOST INTERESTING AND THE BEST WAY TO SUM IT ALL UP IS IN THE WORDS OF THAT OLD SONG:

"IF YOUR HEIFER GNAWS A GOAT IT
SEES IN THAILAND ITS ONLY BY
THE CAUSING OF FRAYED HAY

YOU CAN SIT AND WATCH THE
MOORHEN RACE OVER GORDON
AND TO SEE HIS - SON GROW
DOWN ON GELDED BAYS

IF YOUR HEIFER CLAWS A GOAT IT SEES
IN THAILAND - ITS ~~AND~~ ONLY BY THE
CAUSING OF ~~FRAYED~~ . FRAYED HAY —

AND SEE THE SON GROW DOWN ON
A GELDED BAY

YOU CAN SIT AND WATCH THE MOON

RISE OVER

YOU CAN SWITCH AND MATCH

YOU CAN SIT AND WASH THE MORONS
RACE OVER GORDON

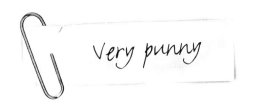

Very punny

A couple of years ago I fled from the city and bought a farm in a remote valley on the Pennines. I tried to introduce Lancashire-bred cows to a Yorkshire bull, but I had to give it up. They didn't like their 'udders feeled'. The only success I had was in mating a young goat with a frozen bottom with an owl with no beak. Mind you, all I got was was a dead-end kid who didn't give a hoot. On top of everything else, my female pig got done by an old ram and within two weeks it was covered in hair and was going round shouting, 'Baaacon.'

I was so lonely, my only friend was an old bendy toy that I found in the cowshed. I used to talk to it night after night as we sat and watched the termites crawling all over the kitchen table and across the bags of grain in the silo. And that's when I found myself singing a song that was destined to become one of the world's greatest ballads. You remember it, it goes:

'Oh bendy toy, termites, termites are crawling. Across the grain and down the moulting swine.'

○ ○ ○○

Many years ago, a half-breed Indian came to this country and became the all-England jousting champion and was chief bodyguard to King Arthur at Camelot. He only had one fault. He would insist on brewing his own beer. He used to keep a big iron cauldron on the boil all day on his window ledge and although the king warned him about the stuff catching fire and spilling over he took no notice.

One day, a deep-sea diver was towing skiffs full of wheat up the river when the homemade booze caught fire and went all over the wheat skiffs and burnt them up. The diver was so mad he challenged the half-breed to a joust with lances. King Arthur was delighted at the prospect of the fight and what he told Queen Guinevere later became part of a song that Vera Lynn made famous, and it goes:

'Half-breed's booze boiled over the wheat skiffs of diver tomorrow. Such a joust they'll see.'

Les with the leader of the Red Arrows.

His mother used to do a strip tease in a bucket of ferrets and his father blew omlettes through his y-fronts. At the age of thirty-seven he ran away from home and married a German U-boat captain called Asa. She used to shoot sailors at Portsmouth and bake them into meat and potato pies. He wrote his song about it and called it 'Asa You with the Tars in Your Pies'.

He died in 1949 during the Glossop fish festival riots in India, when a Morris dancer with a bad leg shot him up the Khyber. This is the song that he wrote as he lay tragically dying ... then he died. He wrote many lovely pieces. Who can forget 'There was a Young Man from Bombay'? Do you recall this chart topper? 'My Aunty Fanny by Mistake'. And then in the twilight of his years he wrote: 'My Dear Wife Swallowed a Pocket Watch'. Oh, the list is endless. The older ones in the audience will surely remember the one he wrote for severely constipated people: 'We Shall Not, We Shall Not be Moved'.

○ ○ ○ ○

Fingers of damp mountain mist curled in treachery around my stout gaiters as I toiled heavily across the bleak ridge of the lofty Pennines plateau. A bitter sullen wind under leaden skies whipped the snow flurries into a maddened fandango of white-flaked fury that crusted my vision to an aching blur and frosted my numbed lips.

At that moment in time, I confess that panic gripped my tripes. After all, I was alone, lost and I'd dropped my cucumber sandwiches. Suddenly, from behind a heap of age-pitted stones, loomed an ill-painted door. I tottered towards it, silently crying, 'Sanctuary!'

I banged on the door. It opened, and there was a little girl, holding a rag doll close to her. The child's hair was a riot of golden curls like ripened corn and she looked at me with eyes that were lagoons of innocence.

'Can I speak to your father,' I croaked.

'My daddy's not here,' the elfin creature whispered.

'Then may I have words with your mother, my child.'

'Mummy's not been in at all.'

I couldn't believe the perfidy and indifference of parents – to leave this enchanting gamin alone in such a gloomy house in this most desolate of places. I couldn't contain my emotions any longer. Falling to my knees I grasped the child to my snow-powdered cape and whispered, 'Fear not little one, I am here now, you are no longer alone in this empty house.'

The little girl looked down at me with trembling lips and said, 'This isn't the house, it's the lavatory.'

○ ○ ○ ○

I straddled the apex of the nameless mountain and the world yawned below my feet in a multi-hued counterpane of slumbering meadow and vale, whose wavering contours were diffused and fragmented by wisps of scudding nimbus that tracered across the azure sky in dreamy vapours.

The mighty, soaring peaks, their massive heads powdered in wreaths of shimmering snow, formed a frowning backcloth softened only by the rays of a watery sun that bled its pallid warmth atop the timeless summits and into the shrouded valleys. The silence was as profound as an absolute zero and the rich, scented air made foolish the senses. My guide and companion, a sturdy mountain shepherd, leaned heavily on his crook and his weather-creased face betrayed his emotions at the sight of such beauty etched from infinity by the supreme architect. His devoted sheepdog too was unable to settle in the face of such loveliness. It would sit, whine, then stand on its back legs again and again. I turned to the shepherd and said in a voice that sounded like a thousand winds dashed on the rocks beneath us, 'Rover is restless. Is he aware in some way of the handiwork of God?'

'No,' replied the shepherd. 'He's got a boil on his arse.'

<u>The columnist</u>

Every newspaper man has a nose for a good story and some two months ago, a sheaf of grimy papers was thrust into my hand by an orphan in Openshaw. Imagine my emotion upon scrutinising them and finding the papers to be an account of the last known movements of one of Britain's unsung heroes – Harcourt Frolic, ex-gun runner, bouncer at Mothercare and stunt man in *Crossroads*.

For years his disappearance was the talk of the explorers' club in Hulme. Now at last I had in my possession the key to the riddle. His marriage to an insane chambermaid from Stoke didn't last. She lied to him and he ran away to sea with an effeminate draughtsman. The ship struck a reef and floundered off the coast of Tortuga.

A native girl looked after him, made him homemade beer and rolled cigarettes for him. One night, when he had recovered, she came to his mud hut. She was naked, the moonlight shimmering on her nubile body. She whispered, 'Now we play a game,' and Frolic said, 'Don't tell me you've got a dart board as well?'

There is a gap in the letters, but in 1946 it appears he cured a militant thatcher's niece from the habit of biting her nails – he hid her teeth. She was so grateful, she got him an audition for *New Faces* but Hughie Green, presenter, bit his lip. Then in 1954 he attempted to cross the Sahara desert without paying VAT and in the last pages of this pulse-pounding saga is the solution to the mystery of the Harcourt Frolic affair:

Monday 10 June, 1954

Oh this heat, the flies, no water left and only one change of shorts. I'm alone, all my friends have gone to a dance in Twickenham.

Tuesday 11 June, 1954

Can't go on much longer. My senses reel under the pitiless sun and my ears were pierced against my will by a jeweller who can't get a mortgage. Threw my truss at a vulture and now I'm really beginning to sag. The end is nigh, the dark wings hover.

Wednesday 12 June, 1954

Half-day closing.

○ ○○○

That night I rode into Tombstone. I broke my big toe
on it. I lay surrounded by redskins – I'd fell on a
tomato stall. A big bald Indian came up so I sold him
a hot poultice to keep his wig wam. He said,
'You come now to teepee.' I didn't mind, I was
bursting to go. I'd crossed my legs so often on the
trail, my truss was crocheted.

    The Indians said, You cowboy big heap.'

    I said, 'Don't you mean heap big?'

    'No. Big heap.'

    They made me a slave and every time they held a
war dance they'd roll a dinner gong across my chest,
singing:

    'We're rolling a gong on the chest of a slave'.

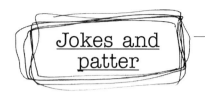

I saw a remake of *Frankenstein*, it was made by British Leyland.
You could tell – the bolt in his neck didn't fit.

I wouldn't say she was fat but she doesn't wear corsets,
she uses baling wire.

She's so thin that when she crosses her legs,
it looks like two wire coathangers in a tangle.

The windows were so dirty they they took the enamel
off the cleaner's bucket.

He drank so heavy,
the only thing that grew on his grave was hops.

When I was a child, I had wax in my ears.
Dad didn't take me to a clinic, he used me as a night light.
(Stood me in a saucer.)

...WE LIGHT FATER - AS SOON AS ITS
LIGHT - SHE SAIS.

The wife bought a chicken last week.
It was so old its beak was crowned and capped.

☆☆☆☆

The house was so damp, they didn't pull it down,
they torpedoed it.

☆☆☆☆

There was a young man from Bombay
Who sailed to China one day
He was strapped to the tiller
With a sex starved gorilla
And China's a bloody long way

☆☆☆☆

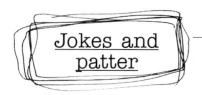

She's so fat that when she passes her hand bag
from hand to hand,
she throws it.

☆☆☆☆

Terrible cough, I've cut smoking down.
Now I only smoke between meals,
last week I had fifty-one dinners.

☆☆☆☆

My wife's idea of a surprise dinner is to take the labels off the tins.
Not a bad idea, but last week I had spam and apricots.

☆☆☆☆

A letter came from the bank. I could tell it was from the bank
as it was written on a wreath nailed to the front door.

☆☆☆☆

The trouble with the wife is, she's ugly.
She's so ugly, beauty treatment's no good.
What she really needs
is redevelopment.

☆☆☆☆

Whenever Father walked in wearing a doleful expression
we could always tell. The dole was full.

<u>Some reviews of Dawson's act</u>

Dorset Bugle:
'The whole evening rose to a high pinnacle
of superb mediocrity.'

Wigan Education Pamphlet:
'His performance certainly taught
us a lesson.'

New Statesman:
'Crap.'

Wiltshire Clarion:
Only one thing spoilt his act –
the seats faced the stage.'

Notes CHARLOTTE EMILY LESLEY.

BORN OCTOBER 3RD 1992 AT 2·40PM.
IN THE SAINT MARY'S
HOSPITAL MANCHESTER

MOTHER TRACY DAWSON
FATHER LESLIE DAWSON
BUMBLEY NAMES:

MOTHER — "POO"
FATHER "LUMPY"
CHARLOTTE "BABABOOBOO"

SINCE HER BIRTH — CHARLOTTE
HAS TRAVELLED TO PLYMOUTH—LONDON—
CHALFONT—ST-GILES AND MANY OTHER
PLACES IN CORNWALL—DEVON—LANCS.,
ETC., SHE HAS APPEARED ON
TELEVISION IN "THIS IS YOUR LIFE"
"GOOD MORNING" WITH JUDY & RICHARD
GRANADA
TV

Personal Notes

PEBBLE MILL MORNING T/V WITH
ANNE DIAMOND AND NICK OWEN.
LOCAL WESTWARD T/V WHILST IN
PLYMOUTH.

CHARLOTTE HAS MET

IAN McSHANE (ACTOR)
CHER (SINGER-ACTRESS)
TERRY WOGAN (HOST)
MICHELE DOTRICE
EDWARD WOODWARD (actor)
JENNIFER SAUNDERS (actress)
LESLIE GRANTHAM. (actor)

SHE IS A BOUNCING BABY GIRL AND
WEIGHS AT PRESENT TWENTY POUNDS
CHARLOTTE GOES EVERYWHERE WITH POO
AND LUMPY AND THEY LOVE CHARLOTTE.
NANNY JEAN BOUGHT CHARLOTTE A
WALKIE WITH TRAIN SOUNDS ON IT AND BABY
LOVES IT —

Scottish Bank Holidays   The term 'Bank Holiday' has a restricted meaning in Scotland, where it does not necessarily signify a national public holiday. For this reason, Scottish bank holidays are differentiated in this diary from public holidays in the rest of the United Kingdom, with the exception of Christmas Day and New Year's Day, which are generally accepted as national holidays in Scotland.

Week Numbering   The system of week numbering followed in this diary is that recommended by the International Standards Organization (ISO), according to which Week 1 is the first week containing four or more days of the new year. Monday is taken as the first day of the week.

The Astronomical Information in this diary refers to United Kingdom and is reproduced, with permission, from data supplied by the Science and Engineering Research Council. Sunrise and Sunset times are based on London. The information given is correct at the time of going to press.
                                                                                                                E & O E

On 3rd October, 1992, our daughter Charlotte was born, and here is something that Les wrote for her as a memento.

And finally...

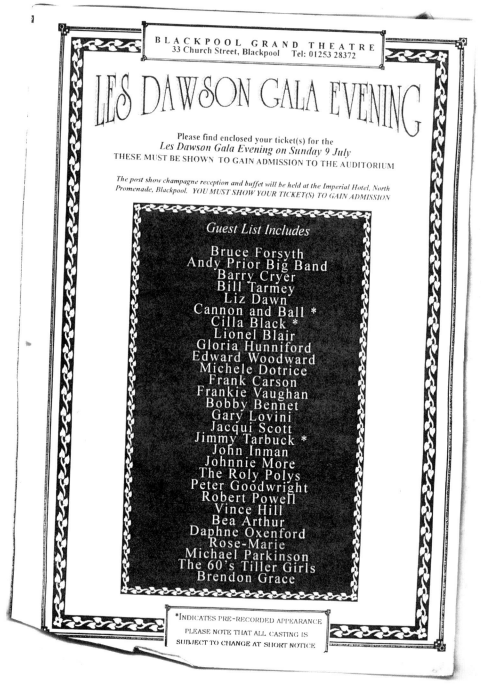

BLACKPOOL GRAND THEATRE
33 Church Street, Blackpool   Tel: 01253 28372

LES DAWSON GALA EVENING

Please find enclosed your ticket(s) for the
Les Dawson Gala Evening on Sunday 9 July
THESE MUST BE SHOWN TO GAIN ADMISSION TO THE AUDITORIUM

The post show champagne reception and buffet will be held at the Imperial Hotel, North Promenade, Blackpool. YOU MUST SHOW YOUR TICKET(S) TO GAIN ADMISSION

Guest List Includes

Bruce Forsyth
Andy Prior Big Band
Barry Cryer
Bill Tarmey
Liz Dawn
Cannon and Ball *
Cilla Black *
Lionel Blair
Gloria Hunniford
Edward Woodward
Michele Dotrice
Frank Carson
Frankie Vaughan
Bobby Bennet
Gary Lovini
Jacqui Scott
Jimmy Tarbuck *
John Inman
Johnnie More
The Roly Polys
Peter Goodwright
Robert Powell
Vince Hill
Bea Arthur
Daphne Oxenford
Rose-Marie
Michael Parkinson
The 60's Tiller Girls
Brendon Grace

*INDICATES PRE-RECORDED APPEARANCE
PLEASE NOTE THAT ALL CASTING IS
SUBJECT TO CHANGE AT SHORT NOTICE

Les's friends and colleagues made this show a wonderful and moving tribute to one of Britain's greatest comedians, raising a considerable amount for the Blackpool Grand Theatre and Arthritis Care.